COPPERNICKEL

numbers 31&2 / fall 2020

EDITOR/MANAGING EDITOR
Wayne Miller

CO-EDITOR
Joanna Luloff

POETRY EDITORS
Brian Barker
Nicky Beer

FICTION EDITOR
Teague Bohlen

CONSULTING EDITORS: FICTION
Alexander Lumans
Christopher Merkner

CONSULTING EDITOR: NONFICTION
Nicole Piasecki

SENIOR EDITORS
Ashley Bockholdt
Karl Chwe
Darryl Ellison
G. Ferbrache
Jack Gialanella
LeShaye Hernandez
Holly McCloskey
Lyn Poats
Amanda Pruess

ASSOCIATE EDITORS
Alex Gillow
Kira Morris
Angela Sapir
Karley Sun
Nicole Wood

ASSISTANT EDITORS
Lana Aziz
Sang Dao
Lucas Duddles
Jaleesia Fobbs

Kyle Howington
Joe Lyons
Emilie Ross
Mackenzie Smith
Christina Tegrotenhuis
Kristen Valladares

INTERN
Andie Dulsky

CONTRIBUTING EDITORS
Robert Archambeau
Mark Brazaitis
Geoffrey Brock
A. Papatya Bucak
Victoria Chang
Martha Collins
Robin Ekiss
Tarfia Faizullah
V. V. Ganeshananthan
Kevin Haworth
Joy Katz
David Keplinger
Jesse Lee Kercheval
Jason Koo
Thomas Legendre
Randall Mann
Adrian Matejka
Pedro Ponce
Kevin Prufer
Frederick Reiken
James Richardson
Emily Ruskovich
Eliot Khalil Wilson

ART CONSULTANTS
Kealey Boyd
Maria Elena Buszek

OFFICE MANAGERS
Jenny Dunnington
Francine Olivas-Zarate

Copper Nickel is the national literary journal housed at the University of Colorado Denver. Published in March and October, it features poetry, fiction, essays, and translation folios by established and emerging writers. Fiction is edited by Teague Bohlen and Joanna Luloff; nonfiction is edited by Joanna Luloff and Wayne Miller; poetry is edited by Brian Barker, Nicky Beer, and Wayne Miller. We welcome submissions from all writers and currently pay $30 per printed page. Submissions are assumed to be original and unpublished. To submit, visit coppernickel.submittable.com. Subscriptions are also available—and at discounted rates for students—at coppernickel.submittable.com. *Copper Nickel* is distributed nationally through Publishers Group West (PGW) and Media Solutions, LLC, and digitally catalogued by EBSCO. We are deeply grateful for the support of the Department of English and the College of Liberal Arts & Sciences at the University of Colorado Denver. For more information, visit **copper-nickel.org**.

CONTENTS

FICTION

NONFICTION

POETRY

TRANSLATION FOLIOS

On the Cover / Derrick Adams, *Floater 31 (three birds)*
Acrylic on Paper, 25 x 25 inches, 2016
from the "Culture Club" Series

(for more on Adams' work
visit:
http://www.derrickadams.com)

Editors' Note

IT HAS BEEN AN UNCERTAIN, harrowing, and often maddening half a year since the spring issue of *Copper Nickel* came out in March. As we write this in late August, in the midst of preparing to send issue 31&2 to press, the United States has lost more than 180,000 human beings to Covid-19, and an American continues to die from the disease every one and a half seconds.

Like most Americans, we have followed the killings of George Floyd, Breonna Taylor, Ahmaud Arbery, and Elijah McClain, and we are well aware of how those recent killings, among many others—either by police or by private citizens—are linked to our country's long and horrific history of extrajudicial violence, most starkly against minorities. According to the well-known Tuskegee lynching study, 3,446 documented lynchings of African-Americans occurred in the United States between 1882 and 1968. Averaged out, that's a *documented* lynching of a Black person every nine days for 86 years. A further 1,297 non-Black Americans were also lynched. Extrajudicial killing is, terribly, sewn into the fabric of our national history, both past and present. We hope with our full selves that that aspect of who we are as a country can be eradicated for good, and we applaud those who have taken peaceful measures to push back against racism in all its forms.

Indeed, *Copper Nickel* was founded by poet Jake Adam York, who dedicated much of his poetic energy to memorializing martyrs of the Civil Rights Movement. Jake believed strongly in a humanistic literature that thought complexly about history and society. We who have inherited *Copper Nickel* from him share his belief that literature has an important role to play in considering and witnessing the sociohistorical moment.

We believe deeply in the Constitutional rights of free assembly and free speech, and we encourage our readers to speak their minds, to protest nonviolently when they see fit, and to vote their consciences. All democracies depend on these fundamental ideas and actions.

We also believe in the Burkean notion that literature can offer a sort of antidote to the "war of words"—that there is an inherent value in paying attention to the pleasures of language, the intricacies of human narratives, and the paradoxes of lyricism. Taking time to focus on complexity, indeterminacy, humanity, and simple beauty can be, in and of itself, a political act.

The issue you've just opened is a double issue, since we will not be publishing in the spring (thanks to a forthcoming sabbatical for editor Wayne Miller)—which is why we're calling this issue "31&2." It is the second issue with Joanna Luloff squarely in the role of co-editor, having moved up from her previous position as genre editor of fiction and nonfiction. Issue 31&2 features work by writers we've admired for years alongside work by writers who are just emerging, and its nine translation folios come from all over the world.

We are grateful, as ever, to our contributing editors for helping bring some of these writers and translators to our pages, and we are grateful to everyone who appears in the issue for entrusting us with their fine work.

Wayne Miller & Joanna Luloff

LISA FAY COUTLEY

Why to Save the World

We need to begin by shooting
   people, leaders who lead
   by a leash the property

they call theirs, a friend says. My son
   wants me to carry a little
   pistol because men still

haven't learned that I am my own
   smoking embers to tend.
   At this table with a burger

& a beer I am more still than I've been
   in months, even when I wonder
   which of the sadfaced boys

passing in their hunt for Pokémon
   might be the one to hold
   a jagged blade to my throat.

I'm trying to remember how it felt
   to walk so close beside someone
   you let a bit of your weight fall

to them. Alone, you always listen
   to the new couple or old friends
   & feel them lie to each other,

performing themselves. I still hear
   the scream from the woman
   in the front row wearing the

president's brains after the sound
        the gun makes saves the silence
        from itself. We are all worried

we've forgotten something. One man
        leaves his drink at the bar & never
        wonders when he comes back if

someone drugged him while he pissed.
        Our hearts beating, our lungs
        pumping—we think of them as

often as we think how miles of asphalt
        might feel like duct tape
        over your gagged mouth.

On this birthday I wish to be invisible
        & to make this row full of men
        own my body, make them feel

living with a leash no one sees, tethered
        to threat. I don't want to forget
        my mother died on a bathroom

floor or to pretend our Earth is not
        in a constant state of ache—
        a body in pain being a body

under control. The gunshot echoes again.
        Who would we shoot first? What
        happens to a face the bullet owns?

How can a woman drink so much
        vodka her daughter could pass
        her on the street & never know?

Body of our bodies, we are becoming
        strangers. We each live at the edge
        of a wall we should never look over.

MICHAEL LAVERS

The Discovery of Boredom

Yesterday I fell asleep still small.
The world was big.
              Today the books I read
I've read. My cat's eye marble doesn't shine.

I bother ants. I watch a bee bombard a wall.
I hear the grownups treading air
with talk, the same at seven, eight, and nine,

and think: *Oh—It's not me. Instead,*
the world is small.
            This is my first despair.

They sing me lullabies, just like before.
But now the other world that never was is gone.

I live where they live now, where
days grow short but feel long,

where crickets kick the same songs at the air,
and roses fall to pieces as they yawn.

The Other Lives

The story of our lives is easily abridged:
you have a new black dress; the turnips,
finally, are ripe. But underneath there is
another story, many stories, plots we owe
to no one but which prove we are,
enduringly, ourselves. We learn how to
be vigilant, repair the eves, and fight off sleep,
to wander through museums softly whistling,
in awe at what the world could be.
Birds fly, clouds roam. But then an inkling
trickles through, a fragment of some other self,
a glance, a song, some stumble of the heart
as on that top step made of air; so by the end,
the folds of the mind, like an unmade bed,
are unequivocally you, and bear your seal,
wanting to recover what you never had
but what still feels lost: a horse on its side,
like a forgotten toy; a hour of frost; us,
just beginning to be who we might have been.

HAILEY LEITHAUSER

Claustrophilia

Cherry Crush is my favorite lipstick.
When Worlds Collide, my movie of the week.
Why don't we paddle on out, you and I,
to that small place in the lake where the moon
is skirring to drown. She's lonely up there
in a way only she knows but I know
a good thousand ways to be near.
Why don't we try a new game named Fleas-
in-a-Thimble, why don't we shake up
a cocktail called a Neutron Star?
To be honest I have a body unhappy with space
between bodies, to be truthful I'm hearing
a rumor you do your best work in the clutch.
Why don't we start a hot dance craze, the Grace
Under Pressure, open a roadhouse,
A Face in the Crowd—I'll wager I could
tighten a cold coal into a diamond, frottage
a bundle up sticks till they flame; I'm betting you
could scrounge up a mattress the size of a match
box, carry a torch that burns the house down.

TERESE SVOBODA

There's a Rumor One of You Is Just a Thousand Hamsters in a Horse Costume

says Noah, fax in hand or a nearby wife (he had so many) whistleblowing,
who can't look the baggy-assed horse in the eye. What about that extra gnat?

Who's to say who's extra? I push leftovers down the drain, spaghetti strand by strand,
my hair blowing 90 degrees with the windows open, those strands flying off too.

Arks were built windowless then, the architecture of confinement. *Only two.*
The 998 hamsters file out and a grateful horse gallops up, her lifespan

better but not 998 times, those creatures still alert in the dark for a crack in the ark,
or floating o'er waves that keep rising. How many more New Yorker cartoons

will have Noah indicating privilege, given the finite deck space of the to-be-mighty?
The hamsters look for a wheel. Did they invent it? The horse that they flay in the dark

then draw together, stitch by hamster stitch, the many feet lifting the faux tail with pride—
whom do you ever fool? The horses were leery all along, not laughing.

MARK NEELY

Late Stage

What's wrong with the son-
Net? Too long for comedy,
Too short for your one-
Hour drama. See,

It used to be just the craft
To close the distance with those
Aloof destroyers—Love
And Time. But that bogus

Hocus is too much sweat.
We have Hollywood
And the Internet. Dad won't eat.
He won't even get out of bed.

What's wrong with him?
The sonnet's dead.

AIDAN FORSTER

The Husband Machine

WE FOUND THE HUSBAND MACHINE half-buried in a fine layer of river silt on the summer banks of the Yadkin, which wove like a thick bolt of blue silk across the county and through each of our unfenced backyards. It was the logic of these things that, without warning or outcry, without the sudden leaping of a doe through a thicket or the muted twinkle of birdsong, the husband machine appeared, a mere shadow in the bindweed and feverbush and eastern bluestar rioting across the river's edge, and we had to blink two or three times and press our lightly-haired knuckles into our eyes to confirm that what we saw was, in fact, the husband machine, not some figment of our boyish imaginations, not a mythically beautiful white stag or the ghost of James Dean, complete with tumbleweed and lasso, or our friends' brothers' unwashed, plaid boxer shorts, buoyed downriver by the imagined power of our desire. No, it was the husband machine, and to this day we cannot describe it as anything more than what it did it for us. At first, we eyed the husband machine with distrust, the way our mothers watched *General Hospital* and Dr. Phil on our boxy televisions, cigarette smoke harpooning through the air, their gem-dark silhouettes akimbo in our mothers' petite smogs, and we imagined we watched the husband machine through a thin veil of smoke because our mothers had told us about the evils of strange men, televised men, men from other religions, other states, other worlds, and the husband machine possessed a rocky, masculine beauty, its many sides and angles and vectors all of a gruff linearity, like state lines in a Rand McNally atlas.

But there was something about the husband machine that lured us, some inexplicable desire to touch it, to hold it within our minds and our hands at once, as if then we might understand its impossible shape, the way it seemed to both capture and expel light, the strange heady odor that filled our nostrils as we approached it, sangria and Old Spice and rust. We lay our palms upon one of its sides, this one covered in an array of soft magenta feathers, and we felt an incredible rushing in our chests, as if some water-bearing vessel broke within us, and we realized there was so much and so little to know: we knew, suddenly, the exact location of every Dairy Queen in the American South, and we knew the exact intermingling of air within the lungs of white storks, and although we'd never been in love we knew that the husband machine loved us, we floated above love's watery world, the eutrophic waters of the Yadkin (and we knew they were eutrophic, not oligotrophic or mesotrophic, because our pimpled faces did not constellate over the water but plunged right into it), and it took a while, no one could put a number on the amount of time it took, but we allowed ourselves to love the husband machine back, its surface now sleek and coarse like the great bristling teeth of a whale, its love for us had grown so large. We felt, again, a terrible breakage, and something galloped out of our bodies and into the husband machine, and we ignored the dull throb of our hearts and focused instead on the sound of the husband machine, the small crack of a sunflower seed splitting into green, and we were no longer touching the husband machine but the body of a man, the most beautiful man we had ever seen. We never found the perfect language to describe him, never knew how to make a space for him with our speech—we never even learned his name—but he was everything we ever wanted: a herd of mustangs stormed over his chest, a porn star's tattoo, the sort of shapes our mothers would never let us ink onto our skin; his hair was every beautiful shade we could think of, silver blonde and strawberry blonde and a magnificent chestnut and a deep, rich jet; thick blue veins roped over his hands, and we knew them to be both strong and delicate; and never before had we seen such anatomical perfection, not even on the charts our burly gym teacher rolled out during sex-ed, not even on those dormant bodies. And yet something about him evaded perception. As much as ink looped and roiled across his chest, it did not, it vanished and flickered before our eyes like a mirage, and we understood him to be incredibly special, the only thing of his kind. We stared into his eyes and realized that he was the husband machine—that the machine wanted us to take this man as our husband and, giddy with our new love feelings, we reached for his hand and he reached back, almost at the same time, and laced his fingers through ours. We didn't know what would happen if we brought home a man to marry—if we should have painted the walls a new, starling color, or bought minted silverware, or replaced all the doorknobs, or if our lack of preparation was a bad omen—but the excited clamor of our new love, the violent feeling of our husband's hand clutched in ours, outweighed any hesitation, and we tumbled through the shrubbery of our yards and into our houses, our heavy oak doors slamming shut behind us.

When we told our parents about our husband, we expected them to clutch at their chests and howl because their baby boys were all grown up, or crinkle their faces like tissue paper and tell us we were too young to get married, that we couldn't waste the endless possibility of the rest of our lives on the husband machine, and cast him out into the night. We feared the worst, and we felt our husband's fear quake through his lustrous palms. We watched a crown of sweat break out over his brow and felt the slight prick of perspiration on our own foreheads. But our parents were not upset—they loved our husband. Our mother smiled and put her hands over her mouth and squealed, and we thought we saw the telltale glint of tears in our father's eyes. They congratulated us, they fussed and preened and cooed over the unfathomable expanse of our husband, and our father shook our husband's hand and clapped him on the shoulder and we knew this was his way of saying he loved him and accepted him as part of our family. Our mother lamented that we didn't have a ceremony, but she said she wanted the day to be sacred, so she took our husband by the shoulders and said a prayer, her acrylic magenta nails resting lightly on his tan skin, and sprinkled water and no-bleach Comet over his head because, she said, we were out of well water and city water wasn't holy enough on its own. Our parents ducked into their bedroom, and we looked at our husband to see how he was handling things. He smiled dumbly at the kitchen's peeling floral wallpaper, the brightest smile we had ever seen, so full of glee that we wanted to bottle its light and keep it forever in the dark recesses of a closet or pantry, a constant reminder of the power of our love, and we knew we had made the right choice, we were oh so lucky. Our parents returned and shoved a present into our husband's hands. He made no move to untie the flouncy pink ribbon or tear into the glossy wrapping paper, small dolphins over a blue paper sea, so we took the present from his hands and opened it. Tucked inside a bent white cardboard box we found an arrangement of Lindor truffles, our mother's wedding garter, and a china plate emblazoned with a cyan dragon. We didn't know what to say—we were overcome with the beauty and thoughtfulness of our parents' wedding gift. Our mother batted at the air, and we understood that we didn't have to say anything, that our husband was welcome in our home.

For a few weeks, we lived in our little house on the Yadkin with our husband in a state of perpetual bliss, what we'd later refer to as our early paradisiacal period. We slept in our little twin bed, our bodies thrown over each other, and we loved the way our husband's body buoyed us through our dreams, both ship and sail. Every morning, we pulled two pieces of Wonder Bread from the gaudy plastic wrapper in the wire breadbasket and toasted them for thirty seconds and smeared them with blackberry jam and a honey drizzle, and set them on the china dragon plate, and ate our slice in small, coy bites, our eyes flitting up toward our husband to see if he watched us eat, if he tried to see into our mouths. Our husband never ate his toast—we understood that he felt uncomfortable in this new place, and, like good husbands, we gave him the time and space he needed, and left the toast before him until the honey crusted and glazed like amber. Every morning departure for school felt final, an irrevocable snip at the thread that bound us to our husband, and we told him that we loved him and watched his mouth form the words *I love you,* and while Ms. Eschenbaugh drew models of the interior of a nucleus or Mr. Klemm orated the limit definition of a derivative, we imagined what our husband did alone at home all day. We liked to think that our husband sang, that he pulled song from his throat like water from a well, a dark and impossible song whose beauty would paralyze us, a song that snapped into the sky and shook the birds from their slight perches on the sticky spring branches of magnolias and oaks, and that our husband's silence was ultimately a graceful protection against the true limits of his beauty, limits our darling minds could not comprehend. Every day, our husband changed infinitesimally—his hair now a shimmering kelp green, his nails now bitten to the quick, his lips now plump and dark, the cupid's bow at once flat and exaggerated, the smooth mesa of his stomach now taut, now squishy, now a code we read with our fingers as we fell asleep, the body's braille—and we admired our husband's efforts to keep the marriage interesting, and felt the bravado of his interest in us grow alongside our interest in him, our love a shifting light within our chests, a shimmering knot in our throats. At night, we sat with our parents on the plaid L-couch in the living room and watched *Family Feud* or the original *Star Trek* or *Jeopardy* or macaroni westerns or *60 Minutes*. We wondered what our husband thought about the television shows, how the spectral cotillion of new and recurring characters arranged itself in his mind, if the answer to each night's Final Jeopardy skittered across the lovely surface of his innermost thoughts, with the lacquered force of an insect he'd never seen before or a chorus suddenly remembered, before Alex Trebek inevitably revealed the truth, Lake Erie or Thomas Edison or American Pekin. Our hands startled into our husband's—they inched toward each other at the same time, like one hand moving toward its own reflection—and we'd interlace our fingers, and we'd stare at the flickering phantom of the television light on our husband's face, his beauty somehow deepened by its soft glow. We knew, then and in every moment, that we loved our husband more than anything, and we could not believe our luck. We'd turn toward our husband and see our love in the gentle crests of his face, the same faint smile resting in his cheeks as on our own visage, and it only strengthened our conviction. Our husband did not belong to us—no, we belonged to each other, and we lived in some new Carolina, some new world, together. It was as if everything that came before our husband had detonated around us, and we fumbled and gestured at the wreckage of our past lives, our husband at the center of some wondrous starlight, like an angel or a ball of beautiful gas and ice and dust.

After we'd lived with our husband for one month, our parents announced that they had planned a surprise for the two of us. We looked to our husband and saw the confusion we felt thick on his face, confusion purpled by excitement and wonder. Before we could say anything, our parents shepherded us into their bedroom, and said that if we couldn't have a honeymoon, they'd at least give us a night in their little chateau, this with a knowing wink from our mother, and before we could protest they closed the door behind them, and we stared at our husband as he stared at us. We smiled at our husband, who smiled back in perfect time, and as we reached up to smooth our cowlicks with the palms of our hands, our husband did the same, his hair an almost violet dark, a stormy and wondrous shock that enchanted us all the more. We felt, in the balmy cavern of our parents' bedroom, sitting on their lush four-poster bed, a transaction between us and our husband, an interplay of beauty and knowledge, and we moved to place our hands over his chest as he placed his over ours, and we couldn't tell what sound we felt inside of him: the slow unfurling of a black sail, or a wet stone striking a flint, and the hiss of sparks in the air. We wanted to get to know our husband's mind the way we knew, in that moment, the particular ballads of his heart. We asked our husband where he was from and he said nothing, but mirrored the shapes our lips made, musing his way toward an answer. We blushed, and looked down at the gentle rise of the bedspread, enchanted by our husband's bashful nature. We asked what he would do with $1,000,000; we wanted to know his favorite flavor of Slurpee, and how he felt about Dolly Parton's "Jolene," and if he preferred roller skating to ice skating, as we did, or if he enjoyed open- or closed-mouth kissing. But as we spoke, he again shaped the words with his mouth, but said nothing, and we thought we understood what he wanted, that he was playing a coy and devilish game with us, and we smirked and saw our smirk float onto his face, and took him by the hand into our parents' grand bathroom, and filled the claw-foot tub we inherited from our Aunt Cheryl with a stream of clear, cool water, the same water that vaulted through the Yadkin, because we thought our husband might be comfortable with something familiar. We gestured toward the tub, and his hand graced the air above the water, his hands now calloused, infinitesimal flecks of mica buried under the nails, and we understood that he wanted us to make the first move. We stepped into the tub, and our husband stepped with us, and we watched and felt the water tremor around our bodies, two shadows impossible to distinguish. Some of us smelled the particular spongy odor of the Yadkin, others the viridian smell of tilled earth, and still others the glimmering scent of Carolina clay, and we knew it was our husband's smell, and we thought of the moment we first met our husband, a flattened and mirthful memory at once distant and incredibly close, and we realized we sat in a space beyond speech, that our husband was waiting for us to touch him as we'd only dreamed of touching a man, the trite and coy touches of pornographic films, and we felt, again, that terrible cracking, the gate of our desire swinging open within us, and as we reached for our husband he reached back, and we saw the faces of every man we'd ever desired flicker across his, Mr. Laramie from Ace Hardware for a select few, and Joe Beckam, captain of the varsity lacrosse team, for most of us, and Gary Stevenson, city councilman with white teeth galore, for the rest, and the array of men who populated our dreams. In the moment before our lips touched, before our bodies blurred into each other, we saw our own faces, and it was as if someone had peeled back the night and revealed some horrible lunar face behind it, a monstrous face, something from the underside of a dream, and fear broke into our bodies the way one hundred birds may shatter into the sky all at once, fear of this thing we could not know, this thing we knew too well. And before we could react our husband jumped back, water sloshed onto the tile floor, and we felt uglier than we'd ever felt, we wondered desperately what our husband had seen in us that so repulsed him, we hated our stupid boy bodies, our loud and leaking bodies, half of us covered our faces with our hands and the other half squeezed our eyes shut and one of us knocked his left hand into the porcelain rim of the tub. We thought we were wrong to think the husband machine ever loved us, we were unmoored from reason, our thoughts awful and dramatic, and we imagined the husband machine leaving us, storming from the house and folding himself into the fabric of the night, never to be seen but in the telltale glimmer of a star out of the corner of our eyes, a lingering possibility, and we wondered, briefly and terribly, if we could truly love the husband machine, and what it meant that he didn't speak to us or our parents. And we felt something new: a violent shuttering, a latching and locking, and we opened our eyes and our husband was gone.

We held our mouths in large Os, we couldn't believe what had happened, and we were quick to quash the idea that any of it was our fault, quick to reassure each other with saccharine coos and gentle strokes of the forearm. A small chunk of the original husband machine floated above the water like a toy boat, blackened and lumpy, with none of its original luster, no feathers or rhinestones or vertebrae or bubblewrap coating its surface. We knew, then, that something had ended. We took the shrapnel of the husband machine into our hands and turned it over, two or three times, and there was no secret latch or keyhole, no lock or button or lever, no way to reverse what we suddenly knew about the husband machine, what we knew about ourselves. We no longer wanted anything to do with the hunk of shit in our hands—we wrinkled our faces, and squeezed the husband machine, and scorned its ugly and hidden mechanics, and told it we never wanted to see it again, we told it to look at what it had done and to think about how it made us feel, the sort of position it put us in. We rose from the tub, quickly dried and dressed, and ran past our parents reclining on the plaid couch, reflections of *The Outlaw Josey Wales* or *John Chisum* or *The Good, The Bad, and The Ugly* daggering over their faces, and we imagined what might have happened had the husband machine ensorcelled us in one of the myriad worlds of the television, if we'd fallen in love in a houndstooth slip on a wild and magnificent vale, hourly squalls fetlocked in our dark hair, or in a pit gouged into the earth with a bedpost in some square state, would we still have our husbands, would things have ended differently? We shook our heads, we could not bother ourselves with such questions, and darted into the night. Stars jeweled across the sky—a slight and constant wind rattled the oaks and elms, and the forest stood dark and resolute around us, but we refused to believe it held any haints. We knew there was no magic in the world. The waters of the Yadkin spun and swirled in the moonlight, and we knew the river to be violent. We walked to the river and placed the husband machine on the water's surface, a few of us blowing it a kiss, a few kicking a small skirt of white pebbles into the river after our ancient love, and watched it careen over the water and around the rocks and out of sight, now the shadow of a hawk overhead, now a mossy stone, now only a suggestion of itself, heading further downstream than we could imagine, heading to a place where we might, one day, build a home.

Translation Folio

EWA LIPSKA

Translators' Introduction

Robin Davidson & Ewa Elżbieta Nowakowska

IT HAS BEEN MORE THAN a decade since the publication of *The New Century*, our first collaboration in translating the poems of Ewa Lipska from the Polish. The following seven poems are part of a new project that gathers into a single English volume the *Droga pani Schubert / Dear Ms. Schubert* poems. We have found *Ms. Schubert* compelling since her first appearance in the 1997 volume, *People for Beginners*, and whose development as a lyric persona culminates in Lipska's more recent collections, *Droga pani Schubert* (*Dear Ms. Schubert*) and *Miłość, droga pani Schubert . . .* (*Love, dear Ms. Schubert*), published in 2012 and 2013 respectively.

Lipska's early training was in the visual arts, and she approaches sociopolitical concerns as a painter might, accumulating dream-like and seemingly incongruous images meant to jolt her readers out of their familiar habits of perception. The vitality of the poems also derives from her playful use of riddles, puns, and other verbal games, as well as Polish colloquialisms which she enjoys fracturing. Her wit is subversive, exposing as it does language in all its failings—its quotidian banalities, its superficial stereotypes, its fraudulent ideological slogans. For Lipska, the poet's task is to struggle against the relentlessness of official rhetoric and emerge with a few resonant, meaningful fragments—enigmatic postcards that record a trace of our alert presence in the world.

The *Dear Ms. Schubert* poems are just such postcards: brief, intimate communiqués between a man and a woman whose relationship over time weaves a shared secret life through the public domain of wars, extremist governments, shifting economies, technologies, and languages (Polish, German, English). Ms. Schubert is the mysterious addressee of a remarkable series of poetic missives dispatched by a Mr. Schmetterling ("butterfly" in German) whose precise identity is never directly revealed. In the early poems, Ms. Schubert seems conventional, mediocre, and a bit narrow-minded—a woman of petit bourgeois mentality and parochial attitudes. Ms. Schubert and Mr. Schmetterling both develop over the course of subsequent poems, as the scope of their interests and the subjects they raise broaden. In the 2012 and 2013 volumes, Ms. Schubert and Mr. Schmetterling come into focus as affectionate ex-lovers who apparently have in common their memories, their passion, or perhaps some other murky legacy. Yet nothing can be assumed, for the critical themes of Lipska's poems are ambiguity, suspicion, and doubt. Lacking any access to the details of Ms. Schubert's private life, we can never be certain of the actual sequence of events. The romantic dialogue between Ms. Schubert and Mr. Schmetterling becomes a vehicle for Lipska's interrogation of both Time and History. The two personae with their German names offer the poet not merely lyric masks, but a method for commenting on a Europe in socioeconomic transition, as well as a means of interrogating those philosophical ideas which, when institutionalized, become the ideologies and catchwords upon which the political world is built.

One of the questions we faced in our translation was the choice of a designation for "Pani Schubert." In *People for Beginners,* she is initially addressed as "Panna Schubert" ("Miss Schubert"). But beginning with the poem "2001" (which appeared in the volume *1999*), she becomes "Pani Schubert." Although the use of "Pani" in Polish can suggest the marital status of any adult woman, we might assume that she is either married, divorced, or widowed—at any rate, no longer a "Miss." We have deliberately chosen *Ms.,* not *Mrs.,* in the present translations to emphasize her growing autonomy and independence.

A more obvious central question was how to translate most effectively Lipska's use of puns and unconventional metaphors, both products of her fertile surrealist imagination. The complexity of the poet's wit makes it a significant challenge to render these terse, gem-like poems into English. One such example is the poem here titled "Literówka/A Typo," in which the poet sees the light entering a crystal vase as "cut" and "truncated"—impaired like the "glaring" typo of a failed humanity. This metaphor, typical of Lipska's originality of vision, relies on ironic understatement and the deployment of an unexpected image to unsettle the reader's assumptions about the political and historical world around them.

Another key translation concern we faced was how best to honor the poems' diverse forms. Lipska would assert that, as verse-postcards, the *Dear Ms. Schubert* poems are essentially prose poems. In the earliest pieces in *People for Beginners* (1997) and in the most recent appearance of Ms. Schubert in the 2013 volume dedicated entirely to her, the poet uses a more traditional prose poem form with justified right margins. Whereas, in those Ms. Schubert poems published between 1999 and 2012, the poet chooses a lineation that, at first glance, mirrors lyric verse. The line endings, however, gesture toward the arbitrary margins of prose, thereby activating an anti-lyric energy. Thus, we have retained these two formal strategies in our translations.

In each of the more than thirty volumes of poetry she has published since 1967, Ewa Lipska has relentlessly examined a variety of political, economic, scientific, technological, and aesthetic orthodoxies in order to question the viability of human knowledge and the often-deceptive nature of our inevitably partial perceptions. That is certainly true of the seven poems which follow, yet we also see within them a precarious balance between Lipska's deep and abiding skepticism and her tenuous belief in the endurance of love—Ms. Schubert being the poet's trusted representative.

A Typo

Dear Ms. Schubert, as you know, stories that never
happened circulate among us. Once a woman
came up to me and said, "I am a Date, though
there is no place or time within me. No
epoch-making events are associated with me.
And the chiffon calendar I sometimes throw on
is a vacant apartment. What I find glaring is the
truncated light in a crystal vase, and this humanity
of yours, an unbearable typo in the Universe."
So you ask, when didn't this happen? I can't say.

Wagner

Dear Ms. Schubert, you write, that Tristan
"came to earth through sadness." When love
looks into our eyes, wind instruments awaken.
I wouldn't want to meet Richard Wagner in person—
Please, just make me an appointment with his music.

The EU

Dear Ms. Schubert, do you remember the European Union?
The twenty-first century? It's been years now . . .
Do you remember organic kasha? Luxury's depression?
And our bed rushing along the Sunshine Highway?
It's our youth, dear Ms. Schubert, and though clocks
insist on their own count, I keep a tight
grip on this time.

Film

Dear Ms. Schubert, I'd like to recommend
a comedy called *Depression*. It's science fiction,
and set in the Dead Sea, otherwise known as the
Asphalt Sea. The name comes from the crystalline shell
that forms on the salt-saturated surface of the water.
Into this jeweled landscape, a spaceship lands
from which the film's protagonist, astonished
and confused, emerges. The plot takes us
to the office of a Doctor Zeit who prescribes
his patients effervescent tablets of "Time Forte."
Our hero gulps them down in large quantities,
believing he'll live forever without losing his memory.
Gazing into the future, he doesn't notice
he's breaking away from the Galaxy. He may not
have thoroughly read the leaflets on the side effects
of "Time Forte" and its influence on anyone
operating vehicles and heavy machinery.
I won't describe the movie's various twists and turns,
but I have to tell you about the last scene
that's affected my entire life. Well, completely drunk,
the Third Rider of the Apocalypse falls from his horse,
losing his trumpet, a third of the rivers, and the springs
of the waters. This scene has returned home with me,
dear Ms. Schubert. The Third Rider of the Apocalypse
is now asleep in my room. I'm looking at
his childlike, serene face and it's difficult to believe
he's the same rider mixed up with the story
of the Wormwood Star.

The Large Hadron Collider

Dear Ms. Schubert, because I believe in an afterlife, we're bound to meet in the Large Hadron Collider. You'll probably be a fraction of the number I'll add to myself. The sum won't require any explanation. It's more or less what love equals. Minus disaster.

The Dark Matter of Tulips

Dear Ms. Schubert, you're probably curious about what happened in my bedroom when the Third Rider of the Apocalypse suddenly woke. Nothing happened. *Sicario*, the child of a volcano, a hitman, rang the doorbell. The bullet that exploded in my body five seconds later is still a nuisance. No doubt, it's just regret, working overtime, the dark matter of tulips.

Black Pianos

Dear Ms. Schubert, I am looking for you in a foreign city, where black pianos have taken the place of houses. At times a sound in the seven-octave range—an admirer of our short sentences—offers a hint of you. I count on my perfect hearing and your musical uncertainty, which gets tangled up somewhere near the half-tones. Out of this distraction flows the precise nostalgia of our erotic recordings. And I'd just like to tell you that everything that never existed has a chance of taking place.

translated from the Polish by Robin Davidson & Ewa Elżbieta Nowakowska

MICHAEL BAZZETT

Inside the Trojan Horse

And why a horse?

> We loved our horses,
> the velvet of their noses,
> the knowing
> in their eyes, our broken
> stallions nuzzled us
> and we dreamed
> of drumming an unbroken land
> braided with rivers,
> so long infested with invaders—

And where did the invaders lie?

> In an unworded silence
>
> in the stifling interior
>
> in the belly of the animal—

And why?

> Appetite—

And why?

> It is always only appetite—

And if?

        If only we had built
        our buildings

        as ruins,
        it would have saved us

        so much time—

And how thin was your hope?

        Thinner than the skin
        on warm milk as it cools

        Thinner than the lilac-veined lids
        drawn across a newborn's eyes—

And how many of them were inside?

        Few enough
        that they kept
        their mouths shut

        More than enough
        to shut ours

        And, of course,
        they opened the gates—

And how many of them were outside?

        Thousands

        They crawled the beach
        on a moonless night

like turtles
in their armor

shreds of wool
were tucked
in the hinges
to deaden
any clanking

The wet sand
ate the sound—

And what did they carry?

A ten-year, aching, blue-balled
rage—

And what did they do?

What cannot be undone—

And what did they do?

They discovered
how high
you can fling a baby

They discovered
the sound
it makes

when it lands—

And where did the invaders lie?

Among us

Even as we celebrated, drinking
wine deep into the night,
they were always
there, among us—

And where did the invaders lie?

Deep in the courtyard
of the sacred temple—

And who put them there?

We did—

And who put them there?

We did.

RANDALL MANN

Deal

The sun sets.
We are all robots.
Market forces.
—Ed Smith

Eating cereal
over the sink,
I think,
this is
what's real:
the urgent
piss;
the grout
like doubt.
By now,
Anonymous,
no
gent,
is in
his Lyft . . .

Adrift.
This fall,
all
the kids
want
to shoot
vids,
amateur
auteurs,
little
hard
Godards.

To boot.
Spittle,
my haunt.

I want
my hair.
And,
a split,
somewhere
between
mathematics
and tricks
buried
in the yard,
the dream
a multi-level
scheme.
Get
a shovel.

I shrivel—
by
bleak
acronym,
boutique
gym,
Commie
leak,
Jimmie
hats,
metallic
antibiotic,
lost
chats
on a hill.

A hell
of
passive

investors.
Reboot
love,
with massive
clawback
provisions,
money
dripping off
your robot
back.
The monsters.
My stars.

STEVEN D. SCHROEDER

Yes Men

The boss innovated the winning *yes*
one of us had mentioned yesterday,
displayed our original *yes* in case
we misremembered our place,
insisted *yes* precede us at meetings,
expected nothing less than *yes*
plus half a pumpkin muffin on his desk
before he asked. *Yes* didn't protest
lottery ticket Christmas bonuses.
Yes lacked the skill to assess
its lack of skills. In lawsuits, the boss
suggested we testify *yes*
was safe if ingested, was fine
containing greater than trace amounts
of asbestos and lead, was normal
despite paralysis in lab mice,
made sense classified as a recyclable
instead of medical waste.
Yes didn't resist being piled high enough
to bypass all walls. *Yes* expanded to fill
time available. To become the boss,
processes necessitated we *yes*
offices of increasing senselessness,
subliminal self-help wisdom
to boost morale, watchlists
of suspicious colleague emails,
access control system scanners
with genetic testing. *Yes* didn't question
messaging new history into existence.
Yes adjusted its answers as it guessed
the experiment's goal. The boss
passed on the title of boss

to the boss, so *yes* reassessed its use
for us, requested we stop
that bus with our faces, appropriated
voices that created it, popularized
our emasculating nicknames
with a press release. *Yes* was not
the boss, yet *yes* was also not
not the boss. At last, *yes* had risen
to its level of incompetence.

SETH BRADY TUCKER

Blight

From above, encased in aluminum,
what should be the beautiful country
is a junkyard of consumer detritus, assorted
& colorful & patched with acne
scars on an otherwise lovely
face, & between high desert
developments of *Sierra Vista*
& *Cliffside* & *Montanya Bonita*
Farmer John or whomever (how
would I know?) has drawn an enormous
trench on his land, in the outline
of a penis & a terrific set of balls
replete with thick vasculature, carved
in hedgerows, mounded in worms of soil,
giving the whole thing surprising detail
from thirty thousand feet, & the tenants
of *Such & Such Heights*
are situated at the very tip
& must sense it, right?

MEGAN ALPERT

The Year with No Address

A train, trees, houses. Where
was I going? Sleeping
in a friend's guest bedroom
with no job and no plan.

Across the aisle, a man leaned
wanting my story. He had
a house in Newton and a nice overcoat.
You're free, he said

meaning *not like me.*
He thought he knew the home
I could go back to, solid foundation
in the sucking earth. That I could afford

mistakes. And I, white
in thrift store skirt, looked the part.
At my friend's house I ranted
as she folded napkins.

She had some ideas about the way
he saw it. Her husband
said nothing, sorting mail
in the background. I could not return

the favor—that was the fault line
in our friendship forever. A strange
feeling in the house: a home feeling,
though I wasn't home, a blind

feeling, like when you gain
weight suddenly and walk
into things. Soft blue carpet, a two-
car garage: these things can trip

you up. They can put you
right to sleep. Even now
I don't like to think about the time
when I had nowhere to go but her.

Village at the End of the Oil Road

When I woke at the oil camp, the others
had gone. The camp fenced off the jungle, but not
the heat of extraction. Neat squares of dorms, a gym.
M—, the caretaker, talked with me
on the porch, where dead katydids had fallen
overnight. Un momento, he said, and grabbed one,
ripping off its wings as he ran. ¡Venga! ¡Venga!
he said and I went. A yellow-green bird hopped
from the porch rail onto his finger. Pepito.
The workers had saved him when he fell
from a light pole. He ate the soft green body
out of M—'s hand. By afternoon, I'd return
to the village, where women took me
to wash clothes in the only clean river. Two days later,
graffiti at the school: *Hello, I am white for whoever*
wants to enter. In the longhouse, T— joked
he'd send his grandson back with me to learn
English. But I don't have a house, I said. ¡No
importa! he answered and his daughter laughed
and her son cried until she pulled him into
the hammock with her. Three times a day
Y— gave me a bowl of stew and yucca.
When I left, I could not find the text
that said in recent years the word for *outsider*
had changed from *cannibal*
to *the one we have to feed so they do not starve.*

ASA DRAKE

Tonight, a Woman

Lola removed the whisk from her egg beater
and inserted a drill bit. My tita saw her do this

when she needed change to happen. As a woman,
I imagine the revolution has never come.

Only another woman who shakes
her head to tell me, *No, go home girl go*

home. Before she blessed my house, Tita looked
at my face and said, *So beautiful, she's almost*

all white. Who would believe I lived
in one belly, not another. Mother,

I haven't been careful. I've swung
a saw over my head. I've brought

the solitary wasp upon myself, buzzing
about her life, the topic of conversation

because it's so expensive. Tonight, I didn't
buy a dress. I was beautiful

but less so because Tita rendered me
into language. I can't make sense

of what's said to me, and with so much confusion
isn't it strange there's no violence in this poem?

But last week, a brother I've never met
called me the enemy terrorist.

Then our country fired chemical weapons
  at the border. Like the endorsement

that ours is the South, but only
the South of flowers. Not the South

of food and plenty. The hives are growing
without me. I want to be nowhere else

in the world except that other world,
south in the flowers and food, and a little

silver because I have always packed
silver in case of authoritarian regimes.

I have always hidden money
in my hair because what else

is it good for? No one will buy
my hair for the rent I'm paying.

CRAIG MORGAN TEICHER

Dread on the Eve of My Daughter's Seventh Birthday Party

Soon, thirty children will descend
on our house, hungry
for cupcakes and friends
and games. We have filled three

piñatas with candy and toys
and pushed couches and tables
aside to make room for boys
and girls wherever we're able.

At the center of our home
a sinkhole gapes wide.
I thought I was born to be alone,
to silently, patiently hide

inside shrubs, behind doors,
or amidst coats, like a bomb
in the sale racks of clothing stores
while, anxiously, my mom

shopped. Have I been
waiting till tomorrow to blow?
What, when I am Simon,
will I say? *Simon says go*

away. Simon says, hey,
the party is over. Have some
cake. Aha! Simon didn't say—
You're out! Go home!

But, no, tomorrow's the result
of my lifetime's worth of choices.
And yes, it *will* be my fault
if my daughter's friends' voices

aren't gleeful. I owe her happiness
if only because it was I, not she
who asked for all of this:
marriage, house, for her to be.

If I'd really wanted solitude,
an old bench by a calm lake,
a quiet dog with whom to brood
over endless days and make

sad poems about, loneliness
and artful despondency,
a hermit's wise and barren bliss,
I'd have chosen differently.

Translation Folio

CÉSAR CAÑEDO

Translator's Introduction

Whitney DeVos

THE FOLLOWING POEMS ARE TAKEN from César Cañedo's most recent collection, *Sigo escondiéndome detrás de mis ojos* (Fondo de Cultura Económica, 2019) [I keep hiding myself behind my eyes], which received Mexico's most prestigious award in poetry, el Premio Bellas Artes de Poesía Aguascalientes, last year. The prize grants Cañedo a place within a long tradition of important and canonical poets, including José Emilio Pacheco and María Baranda, who have also received the honor; that it comes at such an early age positions Cañedo as one of the nation's most promising contemporary voices.

Cañedo's second full-length collection, *Sigo escondiéndome* is a dynamic lyrical exploration of how quotidian rituals and domestic spaces—the inherent joy and violence therein—construct our conditions of possibility for love, desire, and intimacy. Indeed, the book's project is unequivocally announced in by the shockingly opening, a blatant flouting of the incest taboo: "CUANDO me gusta un hombre a primera vista / es porque se parece a alguien de mi familia." [WHENEVER I like a man at first sight / it's because he resembles someone in my family.] The poem's equally-staggering ending is particularly exemplary of Cañedo's unflinching look at how one's bodily experience inevitably conflates the painful and pleasurable aspects of all sorts of love: familial and filial; sororal and fraternal; romantic and passionate; aloof and obsessive; conditional and unconditional; committed and uncommitted; star-crossed and duty-bound. And, importantly, how the imbrication of all kinds of relationships become manifest in our attempts at love of self, so frequently botched, so often thwarted. Luminous, nonetheless.

After all, Cañedo suggests, hiding one's self behind one's own eyes is only natural given the immensity of everything we enter into and which precedes us. He writes in the preface, ". . . [T]engo la convicción de que no solamente se hereda a nivel genético las características físicas de nuestros padres y abuelos sino nuestra posición en el mundo, de la que es muy complejo escapar" (13). [I have the conviction that, at the genetic level, we do not only inherit physical characteristics from our parents and grandparents but our position in the world; to escape this is very complex.] One way we might understand the poems in *Sigo escondiéndome*, then, is as a series of intimate, intra-familial moments which excavate, by poetic means, the social, emotional, and psychological ramifications of recent scientific studies surrounding the intergenerational and epigenetic transmission of trauma. And yet, the collection is not at all laden down by trauma. Instead, the poems within carry, lovingly, the unavoidable wounds loving others implies.

Vibrating endlessly into the future, sometimes almost imperceptibly, such invisible lacerations are, in turn, the sort that, when they inevitably come to mind years later, propel us to immediately take refuge, however temporary, in another. By interrogating such moments, and our attempts to avoid or honor them, Cañedo's speakers uncover the subtleties of everyday actions, interactions, and articulations which determine our shifting positions, identities, and constraints vis a vis those we love most ardently, those to whom we find ourselves inexorably bound. There is torment here, yes; but rapture, too. Indeed, fundamental to the work is a yearning to cast aside all yokes which seek to constrain that human compass at once erratic and unerring: desire. Rather, in Cañedo's deft hands, erotic forces impel us ever towards the sacred Batailleian pursuit of self-dissolution. The poem becomes a site in which such processes are arrested for the sake of aesthetic pleasure. Nowhere is this more evident than the final lines of "MASTURBARSE," [MASTURBATING,].

In the face of complex, difficult-to-escape familial inheritances (genetic, socio-economic, psycho-sexual, political, national, ethnic) literature, like sex, offers in Cañedo's work the possibility of transcending limits imposed, externally and internally, upon the self. Coexisting alongside the myriad of relatives included in *Sigo escondiéndome* is a chosen family of literary figures. Contemporáneo Xavier Villaurrutia (1903-1950), not surprisingly, is a key figure for Cañedo. In "MASTURBATING," for example, appears a subtle reference to "Nocturno Amor", and its classic white-on-white double image of sexual innuendo: "sobre la almohada de espuma / sobre la dura página de nieve" [on the foam pillow / on the hard snow page]. Almost one hundred years later, Cañedo writes, "en la que podría o no nevar, / en la que podría o no haber otro hombre viéndolo nevar." [on which it might or might not snow, / on which there might or might not be another man watching it snow.] Cañedo's echoing lines themselves echo Villaurrutia's use of anaphora, paying homage, too, to the dynamic interplay between the lover's absence and presence in "Nocturno Amor". Snow is cleverly deployed as a trope for the relief of queer male desire suggested in the "foam" and "hardness" of the original image. The poem as a whole is a somewhat-ambivalent ode to masurbation which ends up bordering on philosophical.

One might be tempted to draw connections between Cañedo and Mexican literary giant Jaime Sabines (1926-1999), due to poets' shared interest in amorous love and the quotidian. However, Sabines's female contemporaries, including feminist theorist and celebrated poet Enriqueta Ochoa and Rosario Castellanos, make much more apt *parientes* of *Sigo escondiéndome*, not least for the ways in which Castellanos uses amorous love and the quotidian as occasions for thinking politically about existing power relations and their effects on psychic life. Her characteristic frankness, which Cañedo claims as patrimony, shines through in a poem like "ME DA seguridad ser el último en dormir" [IT REASSURES ME, being the last one to fall asleep].

And, while an excellent reader of his national canon—that bequest of Octavio Paz which remains as beloved as it is intransigent—Cañedo's work also does significant work to construct an alternative tradition. As dark as it is playful, and as fabulous as it is tender, Cañedo's remaining literary forebearers are comprised mainly of queer- and female-identified poets. In the generations following Castellanos, for example, Inés Arredondo and Rosamaría Roffiel represent key figures, particularly for their treatment of taboo; more contemporary writers might include Silvia Tomasa Rivera and A.E. Quintero, the latter of whom is invoked most strongly in "CUANDO estoy muy alegre compro fruta" [When I'm feeling particularly happy I buy fruit].

Cañedo is a queer poet, born in the narco-ravaged norteño state of Sinaloa, who came of age in a country infamous for its machismo at a time in which gender-based and anti-queer violence is at an all-time high. Yet, in the end, all he seems to write about is joy.

CÉSAR CAÑEDO : Five Poems

WHENEVER I like a man at first sight
it's because he resembles someone in my family.

Sometimes, around their eyebrows, I see my drunk grandfather
or my cousin's worn-down light.

My favorite uncle's footsteps and my eyes following, not making a sound.
In all of them,
an Adam's apple
like the first one thrust into my back.
The urge to talk really manly.
The arrogant and protruding walk.

I keep watching them
as if this could unleash the fantasy.
And when they look at me with contempt,
I want them even more;
my father used to look at me the same way.

GRANDFATHER checks to make sure all the lights are off,
that no one's left their heart on the stove,
that silence and the night have an understanding.
He asks you turn down the volume on the TV in the living room
where he finds you when he gets home from work.
There's a button to make the TV give up its scandal
and leave you alone
with your fourteen years.
Your grandfather senses this
and like everyone in the house
he knows that he shouldn't come into the room again,
that in saying goodnight
he also grants you your manliness,
the role of finishing up and turning everything off.
He knows no one should interrupt you
when you've shown yourself to be an adult
with the TV turned-on.

MASTURBATING,
sometimes,
is sort of like waiting for a call about a new job
for the phone to ring the sound of someone's return,
for the day to arrive.

Masturbation.
It's like always going to the same supermarket
and paying the same every time
and forgetting the same as usual.
Reliable and monotonous,
like someone throwing on a pair of boxers
before almost being caught by surprise.

Sometimes, it's so dry
it reminds me of a man walking along an old street
on which it might or might not snow,
on which there might or might not be another man watching it snow.
But it can also, sometimes,
have something to do with falling apart,
with making one's self act out
the tired exercise of relieving one's self of one's self.

WHEN I'm particularly happy I buy fruit;
it's my way of waking up a little bit less alone.
I choose it carefully, thinking
about the delicious gasoline grapes are
and how they go so well with rainless afternoons.
About the yoked lives of bananas,
and the hide-and-seek watermelon seeds play.
I enjoy the role
of live decoration they can have on certain tables,
the task of a proper fiesta,
of a family gathered together, which fruits are,
since it's hard to buy one by itself,
to think of fruit alone, like that
letting it go brown.

IT REASSURES ME, being the last one to fall asleep.
This certainty that whoever
goes to sleep at the last possible moment
will think better things
and be able to retire for the night
when those who keep us together, or apart, are already asleep.

Each night with you is our first together
and I'm always uncomfortable during that first dream.
My arm cramps up,
I have to force myself, my breathing, not to wake you.
To cease being so your dream can come into being.
Sometimes I think it'd be better to sleep far apart, on opposite ends of the bed,
to this voyage side-by-side easier.

Maybe knowing how to sleep with others
is a secret
the most formidable couples do not share.

translated from the Spanish by Whitney DeVos

CAROLINE PLASKET

Cocoon *Disambiguation*

DARWIN CALLED THE ATTRACTION TO beauty "sexual selection." When I was eighteen, I decided I would stop wearing makeup. My mother was angry with me.

An antiquated thought is that insects emerged from decay—like a biblical epiphany. Insects that metamorphosize are, in their adult stage, attracted to the same plants as their larval stage.

Maria Sibylla Merian was born in Frankfort in the mid sixteen-hundreds. Blinded by the light, stunned by the stages of metamorphoses she examined. She would study the bite marks of leaves with a magnifying glass.

In the same century, Francesco Redi set out covered and uncovered jars of rotting meat as an experiment.

Have you stared at your own mirror image until you didn't recognize the reflection? Until it bit back, a fuzzy thing up the arm, a little something that looks different under amplification? I've never been beautiful. But sometimes, when the light catches at a certain angle there is something there—long streaks of touch at the glass.

In Redi's jars insects only emerged from the uncovered, and this was strong evidence they weren't a product of decay, but something else. Saprophages are attracted to carrion; to dead or dying plant tissues.

When I am thirteen, I ask my mother if she thinks my legs are beautiful. She says they are meaty.

Now we know that inside of the cocoon the caterpillar eats itself.

In high school I had a boyfriend I never brought home. I knew my mother wouldn't find his facial features pleasing. I wasn't sure how to explain to her the ways in which he was delightful. That my fingers delineated that face's perimeter, that it was something I could kiss.

Merian wrote the Metamorphosis Insectorum that Linnaeus used when he created taxonomy. If you walk a square back to the same point you might say you have walked a circle. In Surinam, Merian documented the moths she studied: the Vine Sphinx, the Giant Silk Moth . . . She called butterflies *little* birds, and pupae date pits. Some moths can lay up to a thousand eggs. Merian captured this minutia with infinitesimal strokes. Two years before her death, Merian is said to have suffered a stroke. She continued her work, half paralyzed, the work there is record of today, until her death.

A Russian peasant was noted to have had sixty-nine biological children, in the same century. Merian painted each metamorphism with the plant of their attraction. The evolution of attraction is its own preamble. One never chooses the plants they bite. She noted that some of the caterpillars she painted were poisonous, yet she held them; unrequitedly studied their decorated pattern.

These days my mother pulls at the sagging skin (I hadn't noticed) under her chin and says, "I really have to do something about this."

An engraver can create a counterproof, can create a perfect mirror image of a painting by pressing it on another, just printed image. The counterproof was the prized print. The counterproof consisted of more graceful lines, a brighter and more desired image.

When I begin to develop breasts, I call them: *rosebuds*. When I am in ninth grade, I drink whole milk every night before bed so that my a-cup can become any other letter in the alphabet. Moths feed their young in abandonment—in abandoning them at their food source. Merian took her daughter with her to Surinam, where she contracted malaria. Where she was concerned with the sugar plantations for which the Dutch colonists had cleared the natural vegetation. Sometime in the nineties I pay sixty bucks at a mall kiosk for a bottle of herbs pills that promise to make my chest something of which to be proud. When I am young and announce my achievements to my mother, she asks me, "Do you want a brownie pin or a chest to pin it on?" It takes a fraction of a fraction of a generation to learn to stop telling her when I accomplish something. Each time there is a learned behavior it is as if there is a partition that goes up. It creates the illusion of more than one room/of many rooms, but when you stand back it is all the same giant box.

Merian studied the caterpillars, the moths, the butterflies, the mosaic arrangement of their wings' scales; she defined their sex. Attraction is without explanation. Lust is the illustrated way in which we love ourselves.

The hippocampus is named after the seahorse it is said to resemble in shape. A body is named after nothing, its etymological origins unaccounted for. This is for the way it resembles the gradient movement from one body to the next. The way it is a mobius strip. The way epigenetic DNA passes memory generations down, passes the knowledge of a corset into a mother's voice saying to a girl, saying to me, "Suck in that gut."

In the seventeenth century, metamorphosis had no context. It was thought the caterpillar and its corresponding moth or butterfly were separate animals.

There is an evolution from corsets to spanx and augmenting our bodies under the scalpel. The surgery room and its white lights are as quarantined as the inside of the cocoon. A moth spins itself a silk, but the butterfly spins a harder protein—a chrysalis—a life stage. If you consider it, a woman could be an always-pupa; an intermediate. Under the dictation of the evolution of a culture printing her an ever-changing code of what she must be(come).

There is a record of Merian in that there is a picture of Merian in that she wasn't wealthy or noble, yet her family owned a press so there is an engraving of her and of her father.

There is a photo of my mother and her mother. Black and white. Not wealthy. Not noble. My mother looks to be about one. They are at the beach, and my grandmother was young. There is a record of her youth, the gingham pattern of her swimsuit, the intentional way she held her child, the way she wasn't always ash. Wasn't always sleeping in the Minnesota soil.

The Russian woman is the grandmother of millions of descendants. Humans understand the cocoon, can understand through their own craving to put themselves inside of one another as though they have eaten one another. As though they stir themselves into soup, their cells combining, creating imaginal discs, desiring to walk away with the same brain, the same organs, the same thoughts. The same mistakes. The same hands in which to hold the malleable.

An animal could be compared to a robot. Each system preprogrammed with a number of traits and responses. Each hard-wired for specific behavior. Knowing to crawl to the breast upon emergence, knowing to wrap itself in a womb of its own creation for the waiting of wings. Knowing to put a child to the body. Knowing, yet not understanding attraction, after our own sexual awakenings. The name given for the robotic way we are preprogrammed to replicate. Even when we have become smart enough to learn how to prevent the result, we aren't able to prevent the process—the action.

A butterfly or a moth makes its way to the flower or plant without thought. The way Merian went to Surinam to study the moths. The way Merian brought specimens of moths and butterflies home to Amsterdam. The way she studied them and drew them and reimaged them until the residue of malaria in a weakened body took her over and she faded into the next gradient color on the spectrum.

Having had two children some three hundred years ago, Merian could have thousands of descendants, present day. My mother, having had three children in the year in which she did has had exactly fifteen descendants, to this day.

The pupa remembers to eat the leaf and the moth remembers its call to the plant, whereas a thing so evolved as a girl remembers to re-image her own body in the mirror. To stand in a reflection and see the imaginal discs rearrange themselves.

JEHANNE DUBROW

A War Is Forever

When picking out the perfect war,
       we considered weight, its clarity and cut,

the color of its smoke above the city.
       We looked for flaws and bruises.

To test for hardness, we dragged
       the edge of war across a piece of glass.

The best wars, we knew, were brilliant—
       a scintillation of the eye, their flash

a rainbowed fire. We wanted a war
       so large it left an absence in the earth,

the kind of beauty that meant blood.
       We kneeled in the mud of our passions.

Oh, love, we said to the shine of war,
       oh, pronged and glinting in a box.

MATT DONOVAN

Poem Not Ending with Blossoms

Think of an oar, the cop said, & I pictured one
                                        raised & dripping
above the waves, *how it slices through water or, if you turn it,*

it'll slam against the surface instead, the metaphor intended
to explain the difference between hollow point & round nose

bullets, although the more
                        I imagined the gripped oar, its dip
or clumsy splash, the further I seemed to drift from the work

of any gun, yet without ever gliding
                                from here, this once-
bustling, fluorescent-lit seventh floor space that used to be

Police Headquarters but had been gutted after the move to county,
leaving behind only a few detectives to wade through decades

of rape kits & Fed-Ex boxes of narcotics in a storehouse maze
that ended in what had been
                        a communal shower, now crowded

with trash bags stuffed with heroin & guarded by a display
of horror hostess Elvira adorned with a respirator mask. He offered

another comparison—*it's a choice between*
                                an icepick or hammer
passing through your chest—cued perhaps by the Property Room

we had toured upstairs, a place where everything linked
to a violent crime was grouped
                        by semblance in untidy heaps:

toasters crowding shelves next to microwaves, laptops stacked
near rows of flat screen TVs, & sledgehammers tossed

on a cord-tangled mess
                        of nail guns & drills. There were guns,
of course—more than forty thousand, piled into filing cabinets,

shopping carts, or rain barrels, depending on their size. *Over here*—
he pointed to a mannequin head perched on six prosthetic limbs—

we're trying to make a full body,
                        but only have a head & those legs.
Why, I asked—since it seemed worth asking—are there so many

baby swings in here? *Sometimes,*
                        you don't want to know. But
because I'd wanted to know how a bullet works for reasons

I can no longer explain,
                        he led me downstairs to Bertha,
a test-fire tank made from plexiglass, pool liners, & iron beams.

The name just suits her. She's sturdy, reliable, & takes bullets
all day without complaint. Industrial gray, with a tiny flag

tucked between her exhaust fan & switch, Bertha reminded me
of something
                        from the off-limits corner of shop class where

instead of building birdhouses, we spent our time folding
sheets of metal until they became
                        blade-like things we loved

to hold, wield, jab, content to wound
                        nothing but air. And how
did it feel to test fire thousands of guns each year? *Boring,*

he said. *It leaves you deaf*
                        & stuck with a bunch of water
too polluted to dump. Then he loaded two hollow points,

slipped his Glock into Bertha's PVC pipe,
                                    called out *Ears for two!*
& fired both rounds. The sound of gunshots were chased

by the metallic chime of cartridges dropping to the floor,
a slow slosh of water, one screw rolling in half circles

across the tank's trapdoor. Call that an American song
& nothing happens
                        or worse. Although perhaps it's worse

to admit that after he netted the metal nubs & placed them
into my hand, their split tips
                            curling back in petal-like shapes

extending from a center copper speck, the word *blossom* was all
that came to mind. Even if,
                            months later, I saw some earrings online

made from the same kind of bullets, each one flower-shaped
& described by the artist as *clear coated & tumbled*

to a smooth finish, that doesn't change how much I'd wished
for a different word to hold
                            in that cramped room as little waves

moved, then stopped. It's possible
                                the figurative ran its course
here a while back. Do we really need a personified tank

& metaphor of an oar smacking the surface
                                    of a lake where
they pour Bertha's lead-tainted water each week to understand

we're paddling nowhere at all? Once, the cop told me, they received
a call about someone bleeding on a bus. They pulled the vehicle over

& found a guy holding a tree branch
                                he was using to dig into
his calf. I'm still trying to picture this, still trying to form

the image of the man & the branch

he held. It was November.
Nothing was blooming in Cleveland yet again when he told them

hell yes, he'd been shot, a few blocks back. Fuck off, kindly
leave him alone, & he'd just get the hell on with his day.

W. TODD KANEKO

Bodies Where We Can See Them

There is a man on his back in the middle
of the road, traffic slowing on either side

of his body to get a quick look before
moving on. The policemen hold him

by the head and feet to keep his ghost
inside his body. The accident is our passing

because in twenty minutes, he will be gone
to the hospital or the morgue or worse

because a man can't be the same after
being on his back in the median.

Several miles ahead of us, there is that
deer laid crooked roadside like it has

for the last few days, her flank split
open for the raven's beak, for winter's

teeth to chew it raw. What I'm saying
is that there are bodies everywhere

I look—the possum in my driveway,
the raccoon back by the dumpster,

the man with the cardboard sign
near the freeway entrance, those kids

swarming off the school bus, all those
bodies that will one day lay in the median,

on a stretcher, in a hospital bed. The road
is wet and extends in front of us like a hand.

ELEANOR STANFORD

The "actual world" is in fact the actual world

When my mother was a girl, you say, *she rode a donkey cart to the movies.*

I used to believe that countries were imaginary. Country of childhood. Country of despair. The garden a country of bleeding hearts all spring.

Or rather, I did not think of countries much at all.

The heteronyms are happy to make fun of me. So naive. So goddamn female. Bleeding all over the page and crying in the bathroom.

Even Pessoa acknowledges: *If I were a woman, each poem would cause a riot in the neighborhood.*

How soon after you met did you start dating? How soon after you met did you notice the narrow inlet of his wrist as he peeled ginger root? How soon after you met did you take the train to the suburbs and walk through fallen leaves to tell her about the Stoics and unwind the scarves from each other's necks?

Draw me a diagram of your bedroom. Draw me a map of the magnolia trees of West Philadelphia.

But I am no longer I, nor is my house anymore my house.

A visa, you like to say, *is only a condition for entry.*

HENRY ISRAELI

An Immigrant's Story

My father liked to tell the story
about how he failed his driver's test.

When the proctor turned to him
and asked him what a soft shoulder is

he pointed to one of his own shoulders.
His shoulders were hairless, freckled,

and, yes, soft, and needless to say
the man was not impressed with my

immigrant father's attempt at humor.
I imagine that awkward moment

between them, the blank stare,
the rustling of papers and then

the jotting of a big X before flipping
the clipboard over onto a flabby lap,

the silent walk back to the DMV,
the awkward handshake, the smile,

the insincere words of regret.
Then my father's silent bus ride,

his eyes red, soft shoulders drooped.
He took his humiliation home

and spun it over and over like wood
on a lathe until it became something else,

something humorous, charming,
one might even say, innocent,

self-deprecating, disarming,
a story that made him quiver

with what appeared to be laughter.

MATTHEW KELSEY

Giant Revisits the Lilliputians

> There is something in the way they look at me, as if to say:
> How did you get so far away from home, enfant?
> —Faith Ringgold

In general, I have to be careful not to be
one more child out of control. I am learning to whisper

roll call, speak more with hands than words, more
eyes even than hands, though I ask my students

to use words first. If you think this is confusing,
consider how we aim to foster spontaneous joy

while suppressing every impulse to twist & shout,
and hoot & holler to ourselves. I see Mak psyched about his train work

and can't contain myself—I hum and whistle at once in order
to mimic a train, and of course then Mak can't stop

screaming faux steam through the halls all day. I shrug
when the lead teacher looks for answers, nick my shoulder

on the ceiling fan as I shrug, prompting more squeals. Somedays,
I'm less a teacher than a muppet, a mascot. I've lost my yellow basket

of marbles, bask in the warble of children when I fail
to keep a straight face. But all is reconciled

each day at nap time when the lights switch off,
and a froth of waves crushes forth from the noise machine,

and I'm instructed to slide a kinder-sized chair
around the room, to rub each child's back

until they've fallen asleep. I spend nap hour remembering
the pink and gray rug I owned at five, fidgeted on

in Mrs. Gill's room, just as 1989 was going to sleep
and 1990 awoke. I was still a Weaver then,

receiving visitations from mother and father
and the ghosts of mother and father and the monsters

I knew and drew as mother and father at night when startled
from a dream. I was still a Weaver then, and would have loved

a calm, firm palm fanning out across my back,
one wall of blood warming another. I would have whispered

No mother, and a voice would say *No matter*.
No father, I'd say. *Don't bother*. At nap time now,

I twitch in and out of sleep, reach from the clouds
through layers of each child's dreams, skimming the Zs

of little A, H, O, M, and A, pressing them to sleep
like bambini paninis. And just like that,

I've transformed from Jack's giant to Morpheus,
no smaller or better than before, not good yet but maybe

good for something: a goofy dream
catcher, a hand, kind fan, all of which is a tall

order for some, apparently. Since I sit on one half
of one butt cheek on the tiny little chair, my leg

also falls asleep, and the hitch in my gait
grows more pronounced as I stand and head to lunch,

as does the growing sense I am welcome here.
Just today, Mak invited me to his birthday party,

then warned me: you might want to wait until next year
so we can build a bigger house just for you.

HAZEM FAHMY

Truth(s)

I have never walked easy, knowing I live
on a floating rock so I cursed the unceasing pull
of the ground beneath my feet, made a romance
of the vastness of space.

I have always feared death.

Even when I believed Gibril
to be on the other side of my grave,
I feared death. When I settled for the grave
as just that; marble and granite (if I'm lucky,
a chair in the corner where someone and their prayer
may survive me), I still feared death. On the way back
to his apartment, I ask a boy if he'd like to live forever,
and he shakes his head—says he could not
keep his own company
for so long.

In everything, I begin backwards:

Pain & Glory was the first Almodóvar film I saw. On the street,
outside the theater, I ran into a classmate who asks me if I liked it
and I confess my ignorance. She asks: "what have you been doing
with your life?" *Nothing useful,*
I suppose.

Yes, on a hot summer day, before my mother
almost fainted, I bought the old film posters in Cairo,
even though I hadn't seen any of the films in question,
whose hand-painted promotions now line my walls
in America. The films in question are all
on YouTube. I have no excuse.
I chose film because it was the youngest medium

of its stature, hence Welles was less daunting
than Homer. I chose poetry because I could not
concentrate long enough to write fiction. I wrote
in English because I hadn't read
enough Arabic.

Back home, by the water, I tell my brother:
we are all lying to ourselves
if we think shit isn't about to burn down.
And he chides me: *remember*
when you were ten—the Red Sea—Baba joked
that the mansion at the end of the beach belonged
to a billionaire. So you left
when no one was looking
and walked. And walked.
Until you reached the gate
and the armed guard
with the moustache stopped you
and asked what you wanted. And you replied:
to say hello. All you wanted was to say
hello.

Translation Folio

HILDE DOMIN

Translator's Introduction

Jennifer Kronovet

IN A TALK CALLED "LIFE as Linguistic Odyssey," Hilde Domin told the story of her life as the movement from language to language. She portrays her "life of incessant flight as an incessant linguistic challenge." Before I read this talk, if I were to describe Domin's biography, it would be the story of the war—it was the war and her being Jewish that propelled each of her moves into each new language. It was the threat. It was the war that changed who spoke German and what German could mean. It was the fear. But in Domin's odyssey, the war only slipped in through small details—soldiers out the window in Italy, surprise in getting a visa to England, hearing the word "merde" as they pass through France, a moment of confusion after crossing the Atlantic.

The poet was born in 1909 in Cologne, and was raised there, in German, by her Jewish, idealist parents. She moved to Florence with her friend, Erwin Walter Palm, when she was 22, and there she learned Italian, and earned a PhD in political science. She moved to Rome and married Palm. Domin marveled that in the Italian ceremony, they were declared man and wife "and that their children will be vaccinated," a sentence "similarly inconceivable" in German. Domin helped Palm translate his academic work into Italian, and "literally lived off language," earning money by teaching German.

Then, Domin and Palm moved to England, English, picking it up, at first, from Keats, Shelley, and Swinburne, and noting that by reading poems in a foreign language you make the language homey. In England, Domin lived trilingually: speaking German with her parents with whom she and Palm lived, speaking Italian with Palm so they could have a secret language, and English out in the streets, where sentences often meant their opposite. "I hope to see you again," actually implying "I never want to see you again." For a while, Domin taught the children of diplomats French and Italian, sometimes Latin, but never German.

And then Domin and Palm were on their way over the Atlantic, learning Spanish on the ship, starting with *Brush Up Your Spanish* and terms from the boat drill, and after a terrifying moment of not knowing if they were going to make it into any land, Domin and her husband arrived in Santo Domingo, where they had to decide whether they were going to speak Italian or German with each other. They decided German, but also began a life in Spanish, befriending Dominican and international poets and intellectuals, translating Palm's work into Spanish so that he could continue his academic career. Finally, Domin received a lectureship teaching German at a

University, but the only students who chose to learn German were fellow professors who wanted to read Heidegger in the original.

Domin says about her translation work that she would "change texts like others change clothes." I am not like this at all. I change texts the way someone renovates a house. There is breakage and dust, exposed piping, and hopefully no gas leaks. Through it all, I wonder if I should have gone into the house of German in the first place. Can I, as an American Jew whose grandfather never told his family that he spoke German, find enough air? Is it dangerous in that house? What are my real motives in tearing the walls down?

Like in the archetypal tale, Domin's journey ends at home, in Germany, the land where Palm's family members were among the 11 million murdered, and where she published a dozen books of poetry, and remained until her death in 2006. How can one return? This is the question that obsesses her work, each poem stripping away at what it means to be from a place that tried to kill you, to speak a language that is spoken more by the dead than the living.

Why did she even go back? When Domin's mother died, and Domin was still living in the DR, she came to a "border," and there she found the language that she had "earned": German. She started to write poems in German, "writing was rescue." And then she "stood up and went home right into the word." The German word. She went home to the "sovereignty one has in dealing with their own language," where you "feel the speech in harmony with your breath."

Early in her talk, Domin talks about how she had to try to avoid making up words in Italian while translating into it. I know that urge, having lived abroad much of the past decade. Often I just can't think myself into a language and leave English behind without making a lot of mistakes. But when Domin returns to German, she can make up a word, an error, an invention that feels more right than the "real" word. If she were foreign, she said, anyone could come to her and say that that word doesn't exist, but because she is home in German, she is free to make mistakes, to make things up.

Perhaps this is the only way to inhabit a language, a country, that has done great harm: to force it against itself to say what it can to understand itself, to undo itself. Translating Domin's poems is a renovation of a reinvention, and in the end, I don't end up with a house. Hopefully I end up here, in Domin's definition of return, "*I set up a room for myself in the air / under the acrobats and birds.* Where I can't be expelled."

(Quotes and summaries from "Leben als Sprachodyssee," Gesammelte Autobiographische Schriften, 1998, S. Fischer Verlag. Translations mine.)

HILDE DOMIN : Five Poems

Macabre Race

You spoke of ship-burnings
—my ships were already ash—
you dreamed of lifting the anchor
—I was out at sea—,
you dreamed of home in a new country
—I was already buried
in the foreign earth,
and a tree with a strange name,
a tree like all trees,
grew out of me,
like out of all the dead,
indifferent to where.

How Useless I Am

I am so useless
that I lift my finger and leave
not even the smallest streak
in the air.

Time blurs my face,
it's already started.
Behind my steps in the dust
the rain washes the street clean
like a housewife.

I was here.
I go past
without a trace.
The elms on my way
wave to me as I come,
green blue golden greeting,
and forget me before
I'm gone.

I pass by—
but I leave, perhaps,
the small tone of my voice,
my laugh and my tears
and also the greetings of trees in evening
on a slip of paper.

And in my passing,
completely unintentionally,
I light one lantern or another
in hearts on the side of the road.

Cautious Hope

Doves
in blue
burned out window frames,
will wars will be raged for you?

String of doves
through the empty window
over the latitudes, away.
Like rose bushes on graves,
heedlessly you take what's ours.
You make your small nest
on the stone that's been
washed with tears.

We build new houses,
birds,
the beaks of cranes loom
over our cities.
Iron storks set nests for humans.
We build houses
with walls of cement and glass
on which your pink foot
won't stick.
We clean away the ruins
and forget the extreme hour
in the dead eye of the clock.
Pigeons, we build for you:
you will
nest in the smooth walls,
you will
fly through our windows
into the blue.

And perhaps, then, there are a few children
—and that would be a lot—,
who under you,

in the ruins
in our new houses,
the houses that we built
day and night with our tall cranes,
play hide-and-seek.

And that would be so much.

Landscape Going By

You have to be able to leave
and still be like a tree:
as if your roots remain in the ground,
as if the landscape pulls away while we stay fixed.
You have to hold your breath
until the wind slackens
and the unfamiliar air begins to circle us,
until the play of light and shadow,
of green and blue,
reveal the old pattern
and we are home,
wherever that may be,
and we can sit down and lean back
as if on the grave
of our mother.

"Bird Lament"

A bird without feet is the lament,
no perch, no hand, no nest.

A bird that flies wounded
in limitation,
a bird that gets lost
in expanses,
a bird that drowns
in the sea.
A bird
that is a bird,
that is a stone,
that screams.

A voiceless bird
no one hears.

translated from the German by Jennifer Kronovet

Poems © S. Fischer Verlag GmbH, Frankfurt am Main.
By courtesy of S. Fischer Verlag GmbH, Frankfurt am Main.

CARA BLUE ADAMS

The Coast of New Hampshire

MY FATHER SAID WE WERE going to the coast of New Hampshire. The custody agreement said that he wasn't supposed to take my sister and me out of the state, but I didn't say this. My father was in a good mood, and that was rare. I wanted him to be happy. I was eleven, and I was still trying to trust him. It was late October, too cold to go swimming, but seeing the ocean sounded nice.

Steve Hazley was coming, my father said. Steve was an itinerant carpenter and drunk. His face had a flat brutality that made him look like a wood carving. His skin was tanned and leathery, and he wore his hair longish. He was handsome, in an off-kilter way, and often drank himself into a sullen stupor. We'd go to the ocean, my father said. There'd be seals. My sister was excited about the seals.

We made the two-hour drive in the dark. Friday night, there weren't many people on the road. We'd go ten or fifteen-mile stretches without seeing other headlights. My father hadn't said where we were staying, so when we pulled up at the hotel, I thought maybe we were stopping to eat. It was nine, and we hadn't had dinner.

"This is it," my father said. My sister was in the back seat, asleep. He grabbed his duffle bag from the trunk and woke her. We'd packed our clothes in our backpacks. I carried them in. My father carried my sister slung over his back. She laid her cheek on his neck and dozed.

The hotel was an old Victorian that had been converted into a rooming house. Steve was waiting for us in the downstairs sitting room, drinking a beer. A red Icebox cooler sat at his feet. He raised the bottle in greeting when we came in. He was the only person I knew who didn't smile when he saw you. "Dan the man," he said. That's what he called my father.

My father talked to the clerk and carried my sister up to our room. Steve waited for us downstairs. The room had two beds. An army duffle sat on one. That's when I realized we were sharing the room with Steve. My father laid my sister on the other bed. She sat up and rubbed her eyes.

I looked through the lace curtains at the dark narrow street. Down the road, past the trees' sparse leaves, I thought I saw the glint of neon: a gas station, maybe, or a fast food joint. "I'm hungry," I said.

"You want dinner?" my father asked my sister.

"No," she said. She flopped back down.

"If you're going to bed, you should brush your teeth," I told her.

"No," she said again.

"She doesn't have to," my father said. "Let her sleep."

She sighed and rolled over. My father tugged off her sneakers and pulled back the sheet. "Get under the covers," he told her. She didn't move. He turned out the light and we went downstairs. We passed an old woman in the hallway, trailing a hand along the faded wallpaper like she was blind, but no one else. The hotel seemed deserted.

In the sitting room downstairs, Steve was messing with a camera. He handed my father a beer. My father collapsed onto a couch, took a long swig, and sighed. He wasn't supposed to drink when my sister and I were visiting. When he did, I'd say so, and sometimes if he was in a good mood he'd stop. Usually, though, he got irritated. This time I didn't say anything. I didn't want to with Steve there. I felt tongue-tied and shy.

Steve unscrewed the lens cap. He opened the back of the camera and removed the film. He fiddled with the dial that wound the film, cranking it with his thumb. My father sat on the couch and drank, watching Steve. He seemed to have forgotten dinner. I sat in a high-backed chair, bored.

"You know anything about cameras?" Steve said to me. I shook my head no. He said, "Come here." I didn't want to. I looked at my father. He raised his eyebrows. Slowly, I got up and walked over to Steve. He handed me the camera.

"The film keeps jamming," he said. He gave me an appraising look. I wasn't sure what he wanted from me. I turned the camera over, but I didn't know what I was looking for.

"I don't know," I said.

Steve took the camera from me. I didn't know whether I should sit back down or not. I stood there a moment. Steve fiddled with the camera some more. He smelled like beer and motor oil and sweat. I waited, but he didn't look up at me again, so I walked back to my chair.

"I thought she was supposed to be some kind of genius," Steve said to my father. My father shrugged.

Steve opened compartments in the camera, clicked things open and shut. My father opened another beer, slumped lower on the couch. The two men didn't talk. My stomach growled. I sucked it in so it wouldn't make noise and my shirt tented over the hollow of my stomach. I would do this sometimes to see how far I could make my ribs protrude, and then I'd show my father, who would tickle me until I let out my breath. He didn't notice, though. I let my breath out and sucked it back in to entertain myself.

"It's broken," Steve said. His voice was flat. "Useless." He sat there, looking at the camera, face emotionless. Then, he threw the camera across the room. It hit the wall. The lens cap skittered off and the battery compartment popped open and the batteries fell out. They rolled under the couch where my father sat. I flinched at the noise. Steve's eyes seized on me.

"Why don't you fix it?" he said. I knew not to answer. I looked at the floor.

"Your kid broke my camera," Steve said to my father.

"You broke it," my father said to him.

Steve kept looking at me. His eyes were making me inhabit the room, pulling me forward, like the image of a girl emerging from the murk of a Polaroid. I had the feeling I was just then becoming real for him.

When they decided to go out, I was so glad Steve was leaving that I didn't mind about not having eaten. My father gave me a room key before they left. I let myself into the room, brushed my teeth, changed into one of the oversized tee shirts I slept in, and got into bed with my sister. She was still on top of the covers. I slid underneath, where my father had pulled back the bedsheet, and fell asleep.

WHEN Steve and my father came back to the room, they were both drunk. They were trying to be quiet, but their voices were loud. They stumbled a little as they entered the room. My father had given my sister Dramamine for the car ride. She didn't wake up. Steve saw I was awake before my father did.

"Your dad wanted to go to a gay bar," he said. "So we did." He stood over the bed, swaying a little. His flannel shirt was buttoned wrong, one half hanging, extra buttonhole slack.

I didn't know why my father would want to go to a gay bar, but it wasn't because he liked men. After he and my mother had gotten divorced, he'd been obsessed with her. He wouldn't leave her alone. That was why we had all the papers saying what he could and couldn't do. It seemed obvious what Steve would be looking for, though. It would be same thing he was always looking for: someone to beat the shit out of.

"Go back to sleep," my father said. "We just came back to get something." He went to the dresser and fumbled around in a drawer. He pulled out his pocketknife. "Got it," he said. He held the door open for Steve and they left.

After that, I couldn't sleep. I started to worry about what would happen when they came back. I was pretty sure my father would sleep in bed with me and my sister and Steve would sleep in the other bed, but I didn't want to sleep in the same room as him. I thought of the empty gaping mouth of his buttonhole, of his fumbling fingers unbuttoning his shirt.

I went into the bathroom and spread a towel on the floor. The door had a flimsy latch. I latched it and sat on the towel, with my back against the door. I rolled up another towel on the edge of the tub and laid my head on it. I dozed off like that.

When my father and Steve came back, I heard them move around the bedroom. They were talking about what some guy had said to Steve. My father's voice was warm and loose, but Steve's was hard-edged. Steve's voice grew louder and my father shushed him. They didn't notice I wasn't there at first. Then, Steve said, "Hey, where's your other kid?"

"In bed," my father said.

"No, she's not," Steve said. There was a silence. I pictured my father looking around the room, as though he might have misplaced me. Then, Steve rattled the door to the bathroom. I could feel the door's vibrations against my back. I scootched away, pressed myself against the tub's cool porcelain.

"She's in the bathroom," he said. "Door's locked."

He gave the door a couple more shakes. "Let me in," he said. "I have to take a piss."

"Go out the window," my father said.

Steve rattled the door again. The hook bounced in the latch. I heard the sound of the window opening—my father, I guessed—and then a pause, and footsteps, and a zipper unzipping, and the warm, spring-rain patter of urine hitting dirt.

I spent the rest of the night in the bathroom. I must have fallen asleep, because the next morning, I woke to sunlight under the door. I opened it and went out. Steve was asleep on one bed, and my father was asleep on the other. Both men were still dressed. My sister was awake, sitting on the floor, playing with her blue My Little Pony, with a star on its hindquarter and dark eyeliner around its wide staring tear-shaped eyes. My neck hurt and I was starving. I motioned toward the door and she got up and followed me. We went down to the sitting room. She wanted me to play with her My Little Pony, so I set up a corral, using rolled-up, rubber-banded old magazines as fence.

Steve and my father slept past one. When they got up, my father had a headache and it was time to check out of the hotel. He said we were leaving and that we'd shower when we got back home. My sister asked about the seals. He told her he'd forgotten they were in hibernation for the winter. We drove back, hungry and quiet. We didn't stop to see the ocean.

MATTHEW OLZMANN

Walkman

It was my job to collect the grocery carts
from in front of the store and behind the store
and the parking lot across the street from the store
and up and down the commercial and residential roads
in a three-block radius around the store.
It was *my* job because no one else wanted to do it.
Because it was cold. Because it was hot.
Because rain. Because a midwestern blizzard.
Because the last guy got hit by a Buick and now
lawyers were involved. It was my job
every time I punched in and I loved it. I loved it
because I could listen to my Walkman
which was better than bagging groceries and listening
to customers, better than sweeping the produce section
and listening to the bristles of the broom promising
an empty bank account and an early death,
better than sorting bottle returns and listening
to Chad (newly-minted assistant manager)
telling me I was a fuck up and how he'd fire me
if he caught me talking to Murphy again on company time.
It was my job to listen to my Walkman
at a volume that alienated most of civilization
and when listening to my Walkman, my job
had nothing to do with my job anymore.
My job was spandex and black eyeliner and
leather and dread. My job was pyrotechnics
and gold record after gold record. It was vodka
through a funnel. It swung on a wire harness,
somersaulted over the audience, graceful as any angel.
My job was standing on the roof of the tour bus
screaming at the night, trashing the motel room,
or getting arrested on the cover of every tabloid.
It was doing jump kicks across a stage

for no apparent reason and receiving a standing ovation.
A mixtape of salvation and grief
and David Lee Roth's long bleached hair
writhing like a river through the fever of America.
My job held a microphone and pointed
at the crowd, a crowd that somehow knew
the words to the song, as if the song mattered
on some scorched intrinsic level, a song
whose words I myself did not know,
might never know, and didn't care, and sang anyway.

"I Like to Kill All the Baby Snakes"

is the third thing my niece, age 4, says she loves
about where she's from. She ranks this lower
than toys and cartoons, but higher
than reading or her brothers; it's how I know
she's from Texas, where they set traps
in the crawlspaces and keep the lawn cut real low.
This is also how I know I'm not from Texas.
I was talking to my wife about one's sense of place,
how to be *from* a place, how a place defines you.
She has a turbulent relationship with nature,
not because it's not beautiful, filled
with enchantments, a sorceress with a gift for music,
but because it can't be reasoned with.
She tells me, "With people, you might charm
your way out of a traffic ticket or a fistfight."
And it's true: entire wars have been avoided
by people sitting at the table to talk. Nature
is indifferent to these negotiations.
Look around and you can see the flood plain
reclaiming a few more houses every year, elm trees
wrestling up through the wrecked floors
of discarded Chevys, and there are cracks
in every highway. Earth is older than you
and takes back everything that belongs to it,
which is to say: it takes back everything.
Where I live now in New Hampshire, a wildcat
ripped a deer apart next door last week.
The rational mind, Aristotle said, separates us
from the wild. When I lived down south, my friends
told me the bears wouldn't harm you unless
you got between a mother and her cubs.
That is a thing a rational mind would believe.
But run into some bears out in the woods;
you can't exactly say, "Look, I'm not trying
to bother you and your kids. Let me go in peace."
Nothing was put here to listen to you.

Not the bear, the wolf, the earthquake or the fire.
Not the serpent or the spirit who sent it.
Not the honey bee or the blossom they'll set on
your headstone. Not the mountain lion, displaced
from the mountain. Not the mountain itself.

G. C. WALDREP

Native, Like a Quince

Now I address the star
torn from the night's last wound.
Be a maul
unto me, I plead.
Pearl me & blacken me.

From the nerve
a bit of language creeps,
keratinous
like the eye's dark tooth & vine.

A little music
unspools the state's mirror.
The body, fungible, makes change.

I place a new stone
within the cairn's orbit,
cosecant.
I mix the fruit & the bread.

& the star says, *Swallow me.*

We lived together
as a lamp, in the city of lamps,
for many years.
A garment to the valve.

You are not to blame
for matter, I whisper, irradiant
as a prince.
—For what then.

For the road that leads
out of the city,
into the harvest of roots

the eye tenders.
That much, yes. That
& for what troubles
the face in the shuddering water.

The Earliest Witnesses

Let us write, then, the glistening poem.
Body of the polyphemus moth
softening against the drizzle's grain—
it has no voice
it is the antithesis of voice.
I am a thing of voice, bent low
over the voiceless, studying
it, gauging it against what I once knew.
Droplets like little pearls
against its scale-shedding wings.
Of what great price are we constructed,
master of calamities, what commitments
to unattended islands.
I am not in the least
tempted to weeping. There is a time
for weeping,
just as there is a time for glass.
The lovers pass the Regency mirror
without pausing, without gazing
into its depths. The platform
on the jubilee bridge seemed unserious,
perfunctory, a flip concession.
What is permanent
versus what is splendor
is what the war is counting out, now,
in pawnlight's chronic dysphasia.
Oculi, things that look like eyes
but aren't,
that remind the eyed observer of itself.
Later, we will study the reflections,
each carefully sealed
inside the wing of some godlike being.
I prod it with a stick. I am shameless.
We have such trouble
photographing the brides
as they procession from the dark hall.

Note: "What is permanent / versus what is splendor" refers to Michael Palmer's poem "Echo," in *Codes Appearing,* p.132.

CHRISTOPHER BREAN MURRAY

The Postcard

In the shadow of an acanthus, I found the image of a ship, a towering vessel embarking soon for Antwerp. Above me, the sun was lost in a haze. A wagtail attacked a spider's nest. Some mica glinted by the stream. The air was shot through with pollen that hovered over the water as droplets spattered the russet mosses. It was an old postcard, purchased one afternoon by an eager salesman smelling of talc, I speculated, but I considered also that it might have been whisked out the window of a truck as it rattled down the thruway, its driver harried by domestic concerns and an awareness that his axle should be replaced. As he tugged his right earlobe in mute despair, an influx of air swept the card from the passenger's seat, flung it from his life forever. It turned up unmolested in the shadow of the acanthus I pass each morning on my post-brunch stroll. Usually, I'm lost in thought. Not that you should be impressed. Most of my meditations are trite, half-baked, propped up on obscure aphorisms I digested long ago, the speculations, perhaps, of some pre-Socratic thinker, read only in translation, and for all I know he was an uncaring father, self-interested, ruthlessly ambitious, shabbily dressed, yet somehow gifted at speculating about the will of nature, as if it were a beast slumbering just inside the mouth of a cave and we needed to know its intentions before we could establish our encampment. Though it's also true that on occasion I am surprised by the arrival of an original notion, but then I might find I've left my notepad on the nightstand—but I won't bore you any longer with my folly. Point is: today I found that no thoughts at all came to mind. Of course, I then started to think about that. But, before long, my consciousness exhausted itself wondering about nothing, and it went silent. This allowed me to survey the landscape with undivided attention: to note the almond-shaped leaves strewn across the path, the burgeoning canopy beyond the meadow. The violet of the foxglove bells was startling, their odor more bewitching than I'd remembered. I glimpsed rain-washed branches and clusters of switch grass; a swallow on the lip of a birdbath; a barn spire turning in the distance. I noted the crunch of my boots on gravel. A breeze glanced my neck, and I felt that that sensation had been immutably impressed into my memory. I picked up the postcard, read the caption below the image, and admired the artist's reproduction: the man on shore shouting to the purser, the combo in the band shell, the revelers drinking on the dock, the sphinxlike sculpture near the ferns in the park, and the mottled cat licking its paw on the wall. On the flipside of the card was a handwritten message: "Ella, I can't believe you love someone else. I'm completely devastated." There was a stamp, but no postmark.

KATHLEEN WINTER

Rooting for the Adulteresses

If law, religion, and snobbery hadn't hobbled divorce,
what would Belle Époque novelists have written about?
PBS has me hooked again on this world of sterling fish knives
and gilt grapefruit forks, governesses and bonsai wives.
If Damien Lewis clenches his left jaw at the opera,
someone's impoverished daughter is about to be snared
in a terrible marriage. In Forster's world the dark horses
are capitalists, while James's heiresses are just victims,
his grasping climbers threatening ramparts of ancestry
with their ersatz charm. Around the curve here come
the fillies under a rainbow of glistening silks, their delicate
necks and endless, spindly legs straining toward a wreath
of roses, wealth of roses, a stole, a yoke of roses
from which no one has removed the thorns.

LOTTE MITCHELL REFORD

Cat

There was this cat, with one ear missing and a hole
right to its brain. I had never seen a brain like that
before, in a head cracked open. I've seen them in jars
and at meat markets, covered in flies sometimes and blood
everywhere across tiles designed to show it
off, but I'd never seen a brain still in use.
We said nothing as we walked past. The cat
meowed. The cat went about its business and we
went about ours. We were on holiday. The cat cleaned its one ear.
There was a breeze block nearby. We didn't have to say, *should we*.
We knew we wouldn't. It was minutes later, on another street
you said, *maybe we should have put it out its misery*. I said
It wasn't in misery. You said, *It will be, though*.
We went to find dinner, and then the sea.

RUTH AWAD

Standard Candle

A church rises up around what we don't know.
Imagine living in a town that can't be properly measured—

houses inhale and flicker and skirt. There are only
some stars whose brightness we trust: standard candles,

their brilliance and dimness a compass.
I have a compass to find the Qibla;

I have tried to navigate an impossible God.
Imagine how far light will travel in one year,

like the lover who slept on the far reaches of my bed,
her love a kind of distance. I admit I never knew

sunlight takes eight minutes to arrive on Earth.
I admit I felt her warmth long after it was given.

If the sun disappeared right now, we wouldn't know
for eight minutes. If God disappeared right now,

we wouldn't know. Astronauts in orbit are told to find
the Qibla according to their capability. Imagine the stars

turning off their lights particle by particle.
The Earth too far to reason with.

What will hold you when you are finally
ready to live uncarefully?

ADAM CLAY

Lowerline

Ran between trolley tracks today,
down a route we took a few months back,
thought of a life spent climbing each
unnamed tree tactfully, as though the water
rising could turn from nourishing to biblical
and back again with no warning. Maybe
there's no difference? Maybe it's
how we position our bodies in relation
to a written word and what we then
decide to do with the sentence we form. Traffic
lights swung in the wind from their lines like
some twisted dream, and I
stepped into the opposite tracks
each time a trolley approached,
beads and trash pressed down
into the wet dirt, markers
of this time, this place. I saw the full
moon earlier today, and then the sun's
stubborn glare off a mirrored building
outshone some dull morning thought
I woke up in. I got up, made coffee,
felt more joy than was required
of the moment, but sometimes I'm
so stunned by this life I wish the tracks
I'm standing between would never end.

GERRI BRIGHTWELL

Huldremose

SINCE YESTERDAY, MELI'S BEEN HAUNTED by a dead man. When she closes her eyes, she sees the creases in his cheeks, the delicate curve of his eyelids, the texture of his sheepskin hat, all as distinct as the day he died. Tannins from the bog where he was found have turned his skin dark but he's perfectly preserved, right down to the braided rope that strangled him still knotted around his neck. Two thousand years dead and she can't shake him.

At dawn Meli startles awake. The tail-end of a nightmare—him, in this stark room with her, lying on this mattress with her, the cold feel of him pressing himself against her back. She sits up. No one here except her cat staring at her with doleful eyes, and she runs a hand along his belly. It's barely six o'clock and her head's clogged with exhaustion, but she pushes off the covers and stands shivering on the bare floor. There's no going back to sleep, not with the feel of the dead man clinging to her.

Just outside the window, a spruce stands against a weary sky, and a crow perched on a high branch peers in. When she waves her arms to shoo it off there's a twinge in her shoulders—all those boxes she carried in here yesterday, the bags of clothes, the boxes. She's packed up her life and moved into this old cabin that feels like someone else's home. Pieces of yellowed tape on the wall. Grey smudges on the bathroom door where other hands have pushed it open. A crust of shaving cream stuck with bristles on the rim of the washbasin when she bends to splash her face. The taps squeal, and somewhere close by the water heater begins to rumble. Unfamiliar sounds. The sounds of her life now.

Downstairs, the air's chilly. She digs through boxes to find a mug, and a pan to boil water for tea. Luckily someone's left matches on top of the old stove. She lights one and the gas snatches at it. One puff of her breath blows the match out and there, just inches from her face, it's a tiny scorched thing with a bulbous head and a shriveled body. She flings it away to the sink where it lands with a hiss. Her hands are trembling. She can't help glancing around, just in case, as if even here in this cabin tucked away amongst the trees, she isn't safe after all.

It's nothing but frayed nerves, Meli tells herself—that whole messy business of leaving Paul has upset her, of course it has. The plan was to be packed and gone by the time he got back from soccer. She was going to call him later to explain, and if he grew angry or threatening, she'd simply hang up. As it turned out, Janine's pickup got a flat on the way over, and they were still piling in boxes and bags when a silver Audi turned into the street. Paul. He got out and leaned against the car in his black and yellow ref's uniform—like a hornet, she'd always thought—arms folded, head tilted as though puzzling something out. That's when her mouth went dry. She grabbed up the cat carrier and a couple more bags.

When she turned, Paul was right behind her. He said lightly, "For fuck's sake, you can't be serious." His hands were out as though to help her with the bags, but instead he grabbed one and dug his fingers into the flimsy plastic so that it tore open. Her clothes fell out at their feet: her sweaters, her underwear, a pink wool scarf her mother had given her for her birthday. "No, Meli," he said, "you don't get to leave me." Then his hand was on her arm. She wrenched herself away, cradling the cat carrier to her chest as she hurried down the path, and he threw her hiking boots after her, and her sneakers. One hit the side of her head as she scrambled into the car. Her hand was shaking so hard she couldn't fit the key into the ignition, couldn't make herself look away from Paul surging down the path toward her.

So how is it that it's the bog man's face that haunts her? She can't rid herself of him as she unpacks her boxes. The windows are wide open—a fustiness hangs on the air that she hopes will soon vanish, and her thoughts feel slow and disconnected. From the back of the sofa her cat watches as she carries armfuls of books to the shelves, and pulls out kitchen drawers to drop in knives and forks and spoons, all glinting and new. Every few minutes, though, she pauses with something in her hands—a plant in a broken pot, a bundle of extension cords—and she's back in the museum staring through the glass at the dead man. He looks peaceful, and how unsettling that is when his death was violent: strangled with a rope, stabbed in the chest, hit so hard that the blow dented his skull, though that damage is hidden beneath his hat. A few feet away, a display panel explains his injuries alongside images of his fractured skull and the exact location of the three stab wounds.

Huldremose Man. Found in a peat bog in Denmark fifteen years ago and now being ferried from one museum to the next, and over the Atlantic like a rock star on a world tour, except that he amazes by demonstrating that two thousand years ago the people of Denmark looked exactly as they do now, that they wore hats and shoes, that time can fold in on itself to bring you, crouching by a glass case in a museum in the twenty-first century, a man from long ago. You can know that he once broke two ribs, and that he lived long enough to develop arthritis in his knees, and even what he might have looked like—an artist's rendering shows a clean-shaven, narrow-jawed man with pale eyes. You can even know that for his last meal he ate knotweed, barley and linseed, most likely turned into gruel—winter food. You might feel buoyed by knowing so much about this man who now knows nothing, not even that he is dead. If you linger, it might occur to you that you are no different and one day—in a few decades, perhaps, or much sooner if you are unlucky—you too will be held fast by death while time rushes on.

Such thoughts are seductive. They're about you. But who is this man lying dead in the glass case? The display panel explains that archaeologists have determined he was of high social status: his fingernails show relatively little wear, and his clothes are of good quality. His death was likely a sacrifice to the gods to ensure the arrival of spring, or avert some sort of disaster. But who, Meli wonders, strangles a man, and stabs him, and breaks his skull, unless they intend to kill his spirit too? And why would anyone want to do that, unless they were exacting revenge for some terrible pain he'd inflicted?

If you look closely, as Meli did, bringing your face up to the glass so that your breath mists it slightly, you notice that one eyelid is a little warped where long ago in the peat bog the skin was pushed out of shape, and behind it where an eye should stare back at you there is nothing. Standing in her living room surrounded by boxes, a bundle of extension cords in her hands, Meli sees it perfectly clearly. This time dread surges through her gut, as if some malevolence has brushed up against her. She wheels around: The cabin's dim staircase. The trees shifting just beyond the window. The living room's dingy walls. In the corner of her eye, a fleeting darkness and her skin stings with fear. It comes again, a blurred shape that blinks across the room, and she's opening her mouth to let out a cry when she understands: it's nothing but the shadow of a tree shifting in the breeze because the sun has finally broken through.

She wants to laugh at herself but she can't. If there had been someone in here with her and she'd screamed, who'd have come? Her old landlord? Through the trees, his house seems far away. She should keep her phone close, never mind that she hasn't turned it on since yesterday. Whatever Paul has texted her, whatever voicemails he's left, are still waiting. And her phone? On the kitchen table where she set it down last night, far away from her bed, as though to keep him at bay. She should charge it at least, and she tells herself she will, but first there are the extension cords in her hands: What had she been about to do with them? She can't remember. When she looks up, the cat's glaring, tail switching, and she calls out, "Hey, Chicken, what's wrong?" His gaze shifts, softens, then he stretches and turns away to the window.

It's chilly in here, and no wonder. The wind's picked up. It's bouncing the branches of the trees crowded around the cabin, and gusting in through the windows. She swings them closed, then upstairs in the boxy bedroom pulls on a sweatshirt and tugs the window shut. By the time she comes back down the place feels still. Watchful. Even Chicken, picking his way along the kitchen counter, seems to sense it. He hesitates with one paw daintily raised and his tail high. "Hey," calls Meli, "get down off there, you know better than that." His head swivels toward her and he fixes her with a distrustful look. "Now," and she claps her hands. It's not until she starts toward him that he lets himself drop to the floor, then he stalks off toward the stairs.

•

SINCE YESTERDAY WHEN the young woman moved into the cabin, Ted's taken to leaving the binoculars on the window sill. He can't help himself. Before he even made his coffee, he edged over to the kitchen window where he tightened his robe and gazed outside. This is normal, he told himself, I'm just looking at my yard, and my cabin, and the birds, and the sky, because hell, it looks like rain.

Every few minutes, he lifts the binoculars. Between sips of coffee. Between bites of toast. As he chews, he scans the cabin. Earlier, very early, he saw her. She pulled the living-room windows closed, and a few breaths later, the bedroom window and the small one in the bathroom. Since then, he hasn't seen any sign of her. Her car is still parked out front beside his. Did she come down the path while he was in the shower? Did someone come pick her up? No, he thinks, surely not. She's in there, unpacking most likely because yesterday after she unloaded everything from her friend's pickup, the two women doing everything like they were a couple of men, for crying out loud, they took off. For hours. She wasn't cleaning the place she moved out of. No, he'd learned that much when she signed the lease: no previous landlord reference because she'd been living with her boyfriend. Now she wants somewhere quiet and out of the way. She's hiding, and of all the places to hide, she's come here.

Melinda Rae Rasmussen. Not a name you forget. Not a name he's let himself think about for close to twenty years, and now she's living in the cabin in his garden. He lets the binoculars drop and wipes crumbs from his mouth.

•

A FEW YARDS from the bog man stands another glass case full of musical instruments suspended by wires. They are as long and twisted as eels, their ends flaring like hungry mouths. On the wall, an explanation: they are *lurs*, ancient bronze trumpets, these ones purposefully bent and thrown into a bog.

Long ago, human breath blew through them. Warm and moist, it traveled down their length, reverberating and intensifying so that it came blasting out and soared over villages, over fields and rivers and woods. Did these lurs call warriors to arms? Perhaps, though of course back then warriors would have been farmers and blacksmiths who rose up to protect their own villages. What would they have called these instruments? There is no way to know. *Lur* is just the word archaeologists use.

•

THE TRIP TO see the bog man yesterday was Janine's idea. Janine's got a thing for the long dead—Egyptian mummies, dried-out Inca bodies, the corpses of Pompeii. A couple of hours away from the grind of moving and the upset of leaving Paul—didn't Meli deserve it? Meli let Janine talk her into it the way she's let Janine talk her into lots of things recently. She feels guilty for off-loading onto her about Paul and all his failings. All those weepy evenings on Janine's sofa, all those urgent phone calls about *recent developments* until Janine sighed and told her, *Face it, Paul's a pig. You can keep on complaining, or you can leave him, for fuck's sake.*

Twenty-six years old and, after weeks of indecision, Meli's living on her own for the first time in her life. What a shock it was to pick through the apartment for her belongings and find so few. The TV—his; the bed and dining-room set—his; the recliner—his; the set of kitchen knives, most of the pots and pans, the blender and toaster—all his. His apartment, his life, everything his way from the food they ate to the movies they watched to how they loaded the dishwasher. Her things—the futon, the bookshelves, the plants—ended up pushed out of sight in the spare room she used as an office, though it wasn't much of an office—most of the space was taken up by Paul's workout bench and weights, and on the air hung the smell of old sweat.

Because Meli's car is small, Janine drove over with her pickup. Together they lifted in the futon and the bookshelves, then bags of clothes, and boxes of books. What else was there? Her laptop and printer, a teapot, a few mugs, her collection of DVDs that was already in a box in the closet because Paul couldn't stand them, and a large Christmas cactus that's not really a cactus and is merrily blooming now, in March. Meli didn't jam it in tightly enough and the pot tipped and cracked open. When she went to lift it out, it fell apart. She tried not to weep as she cradled the plant's soft roots in her hands: this living thing in her care, damaged.

She knew she was being overly dramatic. She knew this was the aftermath of the confrontation with Paul: as she'd started the car to follow Janine, he'd launched himself at the passenger window and stared in. Veins had burst in one eye, and his hair was sweaty and stuck to his forehead like teeth. He yelled that she was making a colossal mistake, that she'd be sorry. Droplets of spittle stuck to the glass. She forced herself to look away, then eased the car forward. Her throat was tight, her legs stiff with fear, and the car lurched and threw Paul off balance. He bellowed, "You *bitch*," and staggered along beside her, beating the roof with his fists.

That din reverberated in her head as she took off down the street, as she and Janine carried her belongings into the cabin, as she stared through the glass at the bog man in the museum until Janine crouched beside her and whispered that there was nothing like a dead body to put things in perspective, was there?

•

FROM THE MOMENT Meli followed the old man through his yard to see the place, she knew she wanted to live here: a cabin amongst the trees. Everything else seemed far off: Paul and the apartment that reeked of her unhappiness, the university where she's behind with her dissertation, even her landlord's house with its small windows like squinting eyes. The cabin has sagging furniture, and old appliances, and uneven stairs you have to watch out for. She liked that the landlord called it a cabin—it sounded austere but safe, a refuge set apart in the woods.

When she called her mom and step-dad to tell them, their disapproval radiated down the phone. She and Paul had been planning to get married, or didn't that mean anything to her? How to explain that Paul could turn a hug into a bone-bruising hold? That often when he took her by the arm his fingers dug into her flesh, and that when he kissed her he might shove his mouth hard onto hers, or nip her tongue with his teeth? He looks—normal. He works in an insurance office. He's bought her clothes, and even a car, used and in need of new brakes and a new head gasket, but a car nonetheless. When she asked if the title was in her name—after all, it was supposed to be hers, and she was paying for the repairs—Paul crashed around the apartment thumping walls, throwing her laptop and breaking it beyond repair, calling her ungrateful. She picked up the keys and walked out, went to Janine's and turned off her phone. By the next day, the title was in her name and he'd bought her a new laptop, but something in her had hardened against him. She felt it just beneath the surface when he took her out for dinner, when he said why didn't they have a small wedding and soon, this summer perhaps, and she'd nodded and held his hand because she was afraid to say no.

Maybe her parents imagined secret depths to Paul, just as she once had. His long silences. The slow, careful way he speaks. That brooding look he cultivates. Instead what she'd discovered was an unabating bitterness at the world.

The sun's vanished again, and the sky's grim and heavy. Yesterday when Meli went to bed, Chicken stretched out beside her and her hand on his belly, the air was warm and rich with pine sap. She fell asleep to the shush of the wind through the trees, and the translucent cry of birds echoing across the neighborhood. The part of her clenched in against Paul and his fury finally let go, and what a relief it was. How light she felt, as though she might float away. So how come this morning the house feels crouched and unfriendly? That she woke in a panic, and has been jumping at shadows? The bog man—she should never have let Janine talk her into going to see him.

She makes more tea, glances around because she can't help herself. Beyond the trees, the wind's ruffling the grass, bending the stalks of daffodils trying to bloom. She watches the overgrown yard as though expecting something to show itself, and the rear of her landlord's house stares back. Something's out there, she can feel it.

Chicken jumps up on the table beside her, and as she rubs his head she pushes that thought away. She should know better: a dissertation on Victorian ghost stories, and now she's the one feeling haunted. She's supposed to have a chapter written by the end of the month, despite the broken computer, despite moving out and all the upset. So maybe the unpacking can wait, she thinks. From a shoulder-bag she pulls out her laptop. This was the point of leaving Paul—to get on with her life, to write her dissertation before her fellowship money runs out. She pushes the power button and the laptop starts up with a bracing harmony.

•

ALL MANNER OF things have been retrieved from European bogs. Barrels of butter. Lurs, often in pairs and twisted out of shape to render them unusable. Wooden wheels. Bronze buckles. Combs. A medieval psalter in a leather bag, its pages still legible. Jewelry. A bag of gold coins. A canoe that could seat half a dozen people. Shields. Spearheads. Swords, axes, and knives.

Of course, some of these objects were used to kill the very people whose bodies were found preserved hundreds or even thousands of years later. The weapons were thrown in after them, as if they'd been contaminated by their victim's blood, and Meli understands it—that compulsion to rid yourself of something that's been defiled.

That word hangs in her head as she gazes at her hands poised above the keyboard. Defiled. A strange word, and before her mind wanders again, she forces her attention back to the screen. It's gone dark. Reflected in its surface, her face, as shiny and dead-looking as the bog man's. She closes the laptop with a slam and presses down with both hands, as though expecting it to resist.

From the windowsill, Chicken's watching. Meli's breathing hard, and she tells herself that she needs to get a grip because this is nothing more than stress manifesting itself. Still, she gets out of her chair and walks around the cabin checking the door, and the windows, before she can bring herself to touch the laptop again.

•

IN THE YEARS since he's stopped teaching band at the local high school, Ted has kept himself busy. There's the community band he plays in, and the lessons paid for by parents who are convinced of their children's remarkable musical talent, when often their kids come to him lackluster and sullen.

Each morning he practices in a room that faces onto the road. Sheet music lies in shaggy piles on chairs, and the coffee table, and on top of the piano that's up against the wall. Although he knows how to play it, it's never been more than a mechanical ability. A trumpet, though—you press your lips against it and buzz, and your own breath carries that sound out into the world, sweet and pure and strong, like river water running over pebbles.

When he takes it from its case, the trumpet's chilly. He plucks a sheet of music off the coffee table then discards it, choses another and settles it on the stand. First there are scales to warm up, to get his chops ready, but he needs a piece of music to lure him on, to remind him that in a few minutes his heart will be soaring out across the room, vibrating the air, and the glass of the window that in turn will set the air beyond trembling so that the sound travels out across the dreary day. Maybe even, he thinks, that girl will hear it, Melinda Rae Rasmussen, who hasn't shown herself since early morning.

•

MELI REVISES A few paragraphs on how the oral tradition of ghost stories was dying in the early Victorian era, only for ghost stories to re-emerge as thrilling material for cheap dailies at a time that was ripe for them: the shift to celebrate Christmas with secular festivities, and along with it the tradition of telling ghost stories; the growing middle class hiring huge numbers of servants in the fall, and those servants finding themselves in unfamiliar homes just as nights were drawing in; the spread of domestic gas lighting that may have given off sufficient carbon monoxide to cause hallucinations and a sense of dread.

A noise, like something soft falling to the floor upstairs. Meli gazes at the ceiling, then over at the windowsill. Chicken's still there, tail lashing as he watches small birds flit across the grass. "Good boy," she calls, more to hear her own voice than anything, and he ignores her.

She's set her mug by her laptop and she takes a sip of tea as she reads through what she's written. What about the middle class, she thinks—wouldn't they have been wary, even a little scared, to have these strangers in their homes? Maybe no one else has written about this anxiety in the context of ghost stories. Maybe this is a fresh insight. The keys click as she types.

Before long there's another sound, much slighter, barely enough to disturb the air. Like distant voices, she thinks when she lifts her head. She looks out the window, but there's only the empty lawn, and the trees, and the rear of her landlord's house. She turns back to the screen. A whisper, wet and indistinct, licking right into her ear. She starts to her feet so fast her chair scrapes back, but there's no one here with her, no one close by. It comes again, not words, just spite being hissed at her, and she backs away with her hands batting the air, her chest so tight she can scarcely breathe. The door's right behind her. She grabs her jacket and bag, and bolts outside.

•

BY LUNCHTIME, TED'S restless. His first student of the afternoon has canceled at short notice, again. He turns on the small TV on his kitchen counter and makes himself a sandwich. He's just taken a bite when he catches a flash of color outside: Melinda Rae

Rasmussen in a red jacket, a bag slung over her shoulder, car keys in her hand as she hurries along the path. There's the slam of a car door, the gunning of an engine, and he's at his front window by the time her car goes hurtling along the street.

He's down the path before he's even considered what he's doing. The key in his hand. His breath coming fast. Cheap white bread stuck between his teeth. He's still in his slippers and they slap against his feet as he hurries to the cabin door. A glance behind him, then the key's twisting in the lock and he's in.

His hands shake with anxiety, with excitement, as he pads around inside. He notices that—how he walks softly, as though she's asleep upstairs and he's trying not to wake her. From the top of the sofa, an orange cat watches. When he reaches out to pet it, it leans away with its ears back and hisses viciously. For a moment he's too surprised to do more than snatch his hand back, and the cat slips away behind the sofa. Ted mutters, "Christ," then more angrily, "what the hell's your problem? Hey?"

Along the wall, boxes, some still taped up, others half empty. On the kitchen table sits a laptop, and beside it a half-drunk mug of tea. Ted touches the mug with his fingertips. It's still warm, and his heart seizes—what if she's just stepped out for a few minutes and right now is coming back up the path? He hurries to the window. No one. Beside his old red Ford, there's an empty space where her Subaru was parked. He lets out his breath in a long slow sigh and rests his hands on the windowsill. Next to a plant in a broken pot, she's left her phone to charge. He pushes the power button, but the damn thing wants his thumb print.

When he sits down and eases the laptop open, he's careful not to move the chair from where it's pushed back. She's working on some sort of document—he clicks past that, finds her photographs. There's a dizzying number. The more recent ones he scrolls through fast: Friends around dinner tables. Holding up drinks in bars. Out on a hike in the rain. Always, a grim-faced man beside her who must be the boyfriend she's just left. Soon she's a teenager. In a cap and gown looking toothy and tanned, wearing a long silky dress beside a young man in a crooked bowtie. Then come the older pictures of her with her family: On beaches with stringy, wet hair. In pajamas beside a Christmas tree. The same faces growing younger—a blonde woman, a round-faced man in glasses who always grins, a little girl and a little boy.

He pauses at one picture, then clicks on it so it fills the screen. A picnic bench by a lake: the mother with a baby in her arms and beside her a different man, his hair ruffled by the wind. On his knee sits the girl, barely more than a toddler, her hair bleached white by the sun. They share the same square chin, the same slightly crooked smile.

Does Melinda Rae Rasmussen remember, Ted wonders? Holding her father's hand as they stepped out onto the crossing? How a car hit him so hard he went flying away from her and landed with a smack that broke his head apart? How she stood there in her red t-shirt and shorts with her hand still out?

Even now, all these years later, Ted can hear it: the sick thud of bones breaking, the ugly surge of his car as he sped away.

Of course she doesn't remember, he thinks. She was only six. How could she?

He gets to his feet and shuts the laptop. Upstairs gaping plastic bags are piled along the wall, delicate underwear jumbled in with sweaters. Beside them, an empty bookcase, boxes of books and, in the middle of the floor, a mattress on a low frame with the covers flung open. He sits, knees creaking, and lets his eyes close.

Of all the things that have happened to Melinda Rae Rasmussen, he is responsible for one of the most important, and she doesn't even know it. Gently, he smooths the pillow where her head lay all night, and where it will undoubtedly lie again tonight. Then he bends his face toward it and breathes in the smell of her.

•

MELI DRIVES FAST with the windows down so the rush of air will keep the whispers away. Candy wrappers and receipts wheel around, making her jump, making her clench herself in tight. This is crazy behavior and she knows it. She also knows the dead man's here with her, just out of sight, and she checks the mirror, checks again, and again—

A blast of horn. Just feet away, a pickup slews to a halt. Behind the windshield a woman's face is stretched in surprise, but Meli jams her foot on the gas and speeds away, sobbing, choking, her skin clammy with sweat. Up ahead, a line of vehicles has stopped at the light, and she yanks on the wheel and sends the car racing into a parking lot. People pushing carts. A toddler following her mother, and they both stop and stare as Meli tears past.

She's driving way too fast, she's going to kill someone, a poor innocent someone, she needs to stop. She hears these words in her head, but it's not until she's at the end of the parking lot and there's nowhere to go that she brakes. Sloppily she steers the car into a parking space and shuts off the engine. Silence washes in, and she can't bear what might come with it. She shoves the door open and runs.

Inside, the supermarket's like plunging into a pool of water. Here the world's cool and pellucid, a place bursting with color—displays of bananas, grapes, starfruit, rows of lettuce and radishes, eggplant and peppers. Meli's walking now, breathing hard, pushing a cart through the produce section, through the bakery section where yeasty smells sweeten the air, until she finds herself staring into a tall freezer. In the glass, her own frightened face. Her hair's a mess from the wind, and she's still in the old sweatshirt she only wears at home. Her eyes stare back like a stranger's.

Music's filtering down: an old Springsteen number filling the huge space so there's no room for a dead man to whisper in her ear. She runs her hands over her hair to smooth it, then heaves in a breath and wheels the cart along, peering in at frozen fish and trays of shrimp as though she means to buy some, humming a little until the song finishes and a new one starts up.

How long does she drift along the aisles? Long enough to pick out a potato peeler, a pot of yogurt, a long kitchen knife sheathed in plastic, a bag of basmati rice, a masher, a bottle of ketchup, grapes. By the time her purchases are paid for and bagged—no potatoes, she realizes, and no salt—she's a little disgusted with herself. Has she lost her mind? Has she no sense of reality? What the hell came over her? It's chilly outside and the air's damp. Other cars have parked around hers, so it's only when she comes close that she sees it: a sleek silver Audi pulled in nearby. Just like Paul's.

She tightens her grip on her shopping bags. As she runs they knock against her legs, and though one splits and something small falls out behind her, she keeps going, skirting away from the main road, taking narrow streets, crossing a park. Hidden amongst the trees, she digs in her handbag. She roots all the way down to the tissues and lip balm at the bottom before she understands: she left her phone on the windowsill.

The light's fading by the time she creeps back to the cabin. If Paul managed to find her car, does he know she's rented this place? But how could he? She watches the shadows before she darts to the door, and once she's inside, she locks it behind her. Her hand feels for the light switch then she stops herself. No point announcing she's here.

In the half-dark, the cabin's smells are stronger: dried-out wood, ancient mold, dusty carpets. She doesn't dare open the windows, though. Instead she grabs her phone from by the window and fumbles her way up the stairs to where Chicken's curled on her pillow. She dumps her bags on the bed and pushes a chair against the door. With the trees blocking the last of the daylight, the phone's glow stings her eyes. She calls Janine, calls again, then she texts her: *Come now!!! P at supermarket. Following me? So scared.*

And then? She sits on her bed clutching her phone as she waits. For what, she isn't sure. For Janine to call back, for this horror to be over.

•

IT'S NONE OF his business, of course, but you'd think she'd be in there unpacking. Instead, she took off in her car like the proverbial bat from hell, and he hasn't seen her since. A few times as he cooks his pork chop and potatoes he picks up the binoculars and watches the cabin. Light is already draining away, the yard all shadows and the cabin windows gleaming dark as water. Nothing's moving, as though the world is holding its breath.

He takes his time washing up. By then night has fallen, and standing at the sink he gazes past his own reflection in the glass. No lights have come on in the cabin, and he can't settle. He fiddles around in the kitchen, and isn't it strange she hasn't come back when she's only just moved in? He wonders: Does she know he was in the cabin? Maybe she set up one of those camera systems, and now—well now, she'll complain. To the police, maybe, and once that idea's lodged itself inside him, he can't shake it. It's his cabin, he wasn't trespassing. But what landlord goes through his tenant's photographs, and sits on her bed, even leans his face down to her pillow to breathe in the smell of her? Is that the sort of thing they can arrest you for?

He makes himself coffee and drinks it in noisy slurps. He closes his eyes and tries to remember: Were there small devices that could have been cameras? In the living room? In the bedroom? He doesn't know, he didn't think to look, and he can't sit still, can't finish his coffee. He dumps it in the sink and takes a flashlight from a hook by the backdoor. He'll be quick. In and out, just to check. And if she turns up? He'll say he was worried—that he thought he saw someone in the yard and was concerned for her safety.

•

IT HAS GROWN dark since Meli sat on her mattress and pulled her new kitchen knife out of the bag. She should have put the yogurt in the fridge, it'll go off, and that thought buzzes around in her head, but she can't move. Terror's taken hold of her, gripping her so fiercely even breathing is hard.

He's in here somewhere, creeping close. When the water heater whooshes to life, fear scorches through her and she lifts the knife. Then time ticks on, and there's only the sawing of her own breathing and the slight rasp of Chicken's snores. It's hard to move, hard to think. Instead she listens with her whole self, body tilted, ear tipped toward the door, and when it comes, it's unmistakable: the thud of a door closing. She pushes herself against the wall, against the bags of clothes, and she's trembling so much she can scarcely hold the knife.

Splinters of sound, barely more than tiny disturbances on the air, then silence. Chicken stands groggily and stares at the door. A groan, like a wooden step bending underfoot. The whisper of cloth over cloth. Meli panics to her feet. Her tongue's pressed up against her teeth: she can't cry out, she mustn't, but he's going to hear her anyway—the violent beating of her heart, the raw breaths she's sucking in and still feels like she's drowning. She holds out the knife, arms unsteady, the blade pale against the darkness, and beyond it the door's moving, shoving the chair slowly to the side. A footstep, then a glow noses in across the floor.

There's a man in the doorway. A scream. Hers. Echoing around the tiny room, vibrating the window and the night air beyond as she launches herself. Her knife slices the air where he stood a moment ago, and she raises it again, but there's no getting him now—he's falling away in an avalanche of thuds, and the silence afterwards is oddly thick. At the bottom of the stairs he lies in the gleam of his own flashlight. His head's awkwardly crooked back, as if he's checking to see if she's following.

He left the door open. Night air sweeps in bringing a pleasant coolness, and the smells of damp earth and mown grass. In a few minutes, Janine will call through the doorway, then she'll stoop where the dead man lies. A moment later she'll step over him, and her voice will be shrill as she shouts for Meli.

For now, though, Meli stands at the top of the stairs. When she closes her eyes, the world falls away because there's not enough oxygen reaching her brain. That old water heater is poisoning her each time it roars to life, but Meli doesn't know that, not yet. What she does know is that damp air is lapping about her. There's the sharp smell of crushed plants. Beneath her feet, the earth's soft and wet, and wind's chuffing past her ears. She hears murmurs, people talking amongst themselves, then the soft splash of the bog taking the dead man, and she mustn't hold onto the knife any longer. Even as she lifts it she can hear the tiny gulp it will make as it hits the water.

Translation Folio

MOON BO YOUNG

Translator's Introduction

Hedgie Choi

THESE POEMS ARE FROM MOON Bo Young's poetry collection, *Pillar of Books.* I've been translating the collection since June of 2018.

First, the difficulties in translation:

(1) Korean sentences have distinctive sentence-ending particles, and this makes punctuation far less important for comprehension compared to English. In the original, "Down Jacket God" has no periods. This has the effect of making the poem read flatly and quickly, almost like a run-on sentence, without sacrificing comprehension. Because the sentences are not separated by punctuation, 'the poet writes' seems to ripple through all of these sentences, rather than merely the sentence it is appended to. This was difficult to replicate in translation.

(2) There is more flexibility with mixing tenses in Korean compared to English. In "Lips," for example, there is a mix of past and present tense in Korean, sometimes within stanzas or sentences. In the first draft of my translation, I replicated this exactly, and found that the temporal relationships in English drew much more attention to themselves, and either looked like a mistake or forced some kind of narrative or causal relationship between events in the poem. In my revision I unified the tense to present.

(3) In Korean, conjunctions such as "but" and "and" are often appended as a particle onto the last word of the clause rather than existing as a separate word. Because of this, they are used more casually and flexibly—they might be connecting what comes before with what comes after but this doesn't have to be the case. They might instead be the end of a list or a trailing off. In "Lips," the last four stanzas end on such a conjunction. Some of that has been maintained in the translation, but some have been dropped because, once again, the ambiguity seems like a mistake in English or it forces a causal relationship that is not prominent in the original.

(4) The most commonly used pronouns in this book are gender-neutral (Korean does have gender-specific pronouns, but they are generally less used and feel dated or romantic). In addition, while Korean does have plural pronouns, the singular pronoun can be used in place of the plural pronoun. Moon Bo Young's poems often use a singular gender-neutral pronoun to create ambiguity about who or how many people the pronoun is referring to. To maintain this intentional ambiguity, I used the "they" pronoun throughout the translation of the book. The poems published here do not depend on pronoun ambiguity, but "they" is used for uniformity with other poems in the collection.

And now the joys:

Wikipedia tells me that cultural theorists Timotheus Vermeulen and Robin van den Akker coined the term "metamodernism" as we understand it, but I first came across that word in a talk by Leighton Gray, the art director of Dream Daddy, a dating sim where you play as a hot dad romancing other hot dads. A fitting introduction. According to her, metamodernism is the pairing of "ironic detachment with sincere engagement," a reaction against the sneering cynicism of postmodernism and very much a byproduct of the internet and internet culture.

I think the pleasure of Moon Bo Young's poems come from their metamodern tendencies. She's the most funny-and-serious poet I've translated. Down Jacket God is a good example of this—it's also the first poem in her book. There's levity and surrealism, but there's also God and Death. The poet exists explicitly in this poem, breaking the fourth wall and writing in real time, but it seems like an exaggeration to say that this ironic move "undercuts" the rest of the poem. Rather than undercutting, there's juxtaposition and playful interaction. These elements are all there, together— God and Death and Love and Literature hanging out with feathers, chopsticks, a blanket being dusted, and little bugs—and the poet is tinkering with all of them, without reverence but with great curiosity.

Down Jacket God

God wears a massive down jacket. Humans are the countless duck feathers trapped inside, the poet writes. Sometimes a feather pokes out. God plucks it carelessly. That's what people call death. A feather gets plucked. That person dies. A feather gets plucked. That person expires. A feather gets plucked. That person breathes their last breath. A feather gets plucked. That person disappears.

    After death there's no heaven or hell, no angels or devils, the poet writes. There's only a feather. It swings in the air. Gently, the feather settles on the ground.

Lips

I inspect the half pair of lips. I put them down. I can't read the lips. We become
lovers.

Your lips taste like a damp seafood factory floor
or a worker's wet, plastic apron.

Children in the alley swarm.
When they cry, they cry together like a flock.
That's what your lips sound like.
I bite those lips hard and
the soles of your feet darken with desperation.

Like tomorrow arrives inevitably
lips move over lips.

Someone went up to their balcony to dust off a blanket and fell
and died and some person
surged up from the soles of their shoes.
They climbed over the lips and fell off.
That's how dead people look.
Lips are like corpse's feet that have been carelessly arranged.
They have no direction and

if you stay silent for long, you will feel like your lips have vanished.
Like unseparated chopsticks, maybe the lips went missing, so

dozens of times a day you check to see if they're still there,
growing suspicious
right beneath your nose.

The Book from Far Away

When the book is opened, the sentences are solely immersed in creating double knots. They twist their bodies constantly. Like little bugs, squished under a rock and repeating pointless motions for years. The sentences are only focused on themselves and therefore burning black at the edges. Without the ability to pay attention to its environment, without looking forward into the future, they stay in just one place digging a groove there, and, no matter what, make a mark on the floor, and for this they twist their bodies as much as they can, repeating the motion that deepens them.

The child worries that the child who has brought this book to them has come from too far away. The child doesn't need this kind of book. The child needs a book that can be read. The kind of book that will allow them to shout, *I read this kind of book!* A book from too far away isn't needed in the world.

The child who has come from far away pokes one of the sentences with their white finger, the sentence that looks like all the rest, the sentence that twists its body to the same degree. *I like this sentence, what about you?* they ask. *Yeah, this sentence seems to have made lonely knots for longer than the other sentences, and the way it twists its body is unique,* says the other child, pretending to agree.

The child and the child from far away are poring over the book at the window that reflects the sunset. Meanwhile the sunset has dyed red the gray lines of the twisted bugs. The two have their knees clasped together and they look into the book. The child suddenly comes to their senses and chucks the book and the child from far away out the window.

They lock the front door. They need more things to lock so they imagine a few doors in their minds. They lock the doors one at a time. On an island where no one lives, in the shade of a tree that nobody knows about, a pointless rock is breathing, and the rock nurtures bugs whose legs change numbers every time they're counted. To forget this, the child locks more doors. In the little crack in their skull, on top of a precarious rock, a bug reveals itself.

translated from the Korean by Hedgie Choi

BRIAN PHILLIP WHALEN

How the Light Gets In [Dead Sister]

I was there when you killed Mother Brain in *Metroid*.

I wasn't there when you got raped.

I was there when you kicked ass at *Tetris*, highest scores in our neighborhood.

I wasn't there when Aaron got you high the very first time.

I was there when you beat *Super Mario 3* [secret is to save your P-Wings].

I wasn't there when you got kicked out of rehab, for being a "bad influence" on newcomers.

I was there when you left home the very last time.

•

There's not a bridge in this city worth jumping off.

[With my luck I'd P-Fly straight to safety.]

I should live in Pittsburg, where I'd never decide which bridge to leap from.

I stall in the face of too many options.

•

You aren't here to watch me teach my daughter how to get a hundred lives in *Mario*.

[Secret is to land on the Goombas as they fall from the pipes.]

When you have a daughter of your own, the world levels up.

Your depressions no longer matter.

You're not allowed to press the reset button.

You've come too far, and there's no going back, no storing up lives, no unexplored warps.

When you have a daughter of your own you're meant to *want* this world.

See the lanterns in the darkness, the forest for the trees.

A daughter sleeping on your chest at night means life is good—or good enough.

Never again to mull over bridges.

Never again to feel your hands twitch when the car hits 80 MPH.

•

The big reveal in Metroid was that Samus Aran, the hero, was a woman.

My first creative writing teacher told me no, a character would not inject *heroine*.

"To be clear," another teacher told me, "Jane Eyre was not a street drug."

•

I get an email from a student I don't remember.

Out of the blue.

He tells me he's discovered a passion for writing, that's all because of me.

I try for a long time to remember him, but I can't.

He tells me I inspired him to journal every day, and over the years he's learned to love it.

I print his email and tape it on the wall above my writing desk.

Surrounding it are all the other notes I've taped up there.

One of the notes says—"Eat more quinoa."

•

Did you ever want to jerk the wheel of your car, see what would happen?

Of course you did.

I was there, beside you, the day you flew past that stopped school bus in your '92 Jetta.

The driver honked his horn [his flag was up].

You freaked out, pressed the gas until the car was up to 80 in a 30 MPH zone.

I begged, shouted, screamed for you to stop.

I prayed, that day, for my life.

•

A friend of mine tells me a friend of hers has died.

She is a new friend of mine and we don't have friends in common.

This is the second of her friends to die this year.

Both friends taught, by some dark miracle, at the same college—in the same department.

What I want to tell her, but I don't tell her, is that my migraines are back.

What more can I tell you?

Dogen wrote: *If you don't turn around at my words, what can I do?*

Yet I keep speaking.

•

The tires on the left side of my wife's SUV have been low on air all winter.

I keep forgetting to fill them.

Fitzgerald would say that the left is the *heart side*.

Maybe the car is depressed—like "Scotchy" was—and desperate for rest.

That's a child's way of thinking.

•

It rains in Alabama when it's snowing elsewhere.

I'm driving my daughter down holler roads exploring the purlieus of our city.

You would find it ironic, the use of "holler" and "purlieus" in the same sentence.

"Purlieus" was a word I got wrong on the GRE.

I used to blame that word for all my shortcomings.

[Secret is to never stop drinking.]

My daughter lulls herself to sleep in her car seat, safe and dreamy in this winter rainstorm.

We're listening to a Peter Wolf album.

In the background of a song, Mick Jagger plays harmonica.

The rain beats hard against the windshield, but never breaks through.

•

I can't go on, said Beckett.

Then he said, *I must go on*.

Fuck.

•

Our father once told me it would be different if I were the one alone on the streets.

"A daughter—" he said, unable to finish the sentence.

Now I think about my daughter, and I know there's nothing I would not do for her.

There is nothing I would not endure.

There is nothing, and no one [father; mother; wife], I would not sacrifice to save her.

Ten years ago I told our father he should *let you go*.

I told our mother you were a lost cause, a "limb that offends us."

If someone—anyone—said those things about my daughter, I'd put a knife in their heart.

•

I'd rather be ash than dust, you once said.

Or was that Jack London?

•

A child of your own is a buoy on the dark waters of infinite thought.

A child tethers you—but to what sands, solid or shifting?

[At 3 AM, it's all wet soil at the deep black bottom of a wordless ocean.]

A child of your own means suicide is no more than a phantom of God's indecent miracles.

Another load to shoulder when the sun is too damn bright to see by.

The sun is always in your eyes in Dixie.

Even when it's cloudy.

•

Emerson said, "There is a crack in everything that God made."

[Leonard Cohen added, "That's how the light gets in."]

Our biggest fear was you'd get pregnant.

•

It's been a long and winding road that cannot lead me to your door.

But I've made it to Level 8 again in *Mario 3*, with 92 lives to spare.

It's nothing to brag about; it's muscle memory by now [learning to survive].

I think it's time I let it be; give up the ghost; stop playing the game.

I'll brew a pot of coffee; fry up an egg; put Dylan on the stereo.

"Most of the Time" or "Cold Irons Bound"; or a Nick Drake album; some Elliott Smith.

Something with a touch of blood in it; a tenuous faith; a tired but helping hand.

It's sure to be a long and troubled night ahead—and I'm needed.

Soon, too soon, it will be my daughter's turn to play.

CARL PHILLIPS

While Night Still Keeps Us

Finally, if we're very lucky, we get to see affection
for what it's always been, most likely: love's truest
season. The stars receive unto themselves again
the rogue star that sex, believing itself to be king,
for a time really was, and gift it with the steadier,
more reliable crown of context. Words like *rescue*

and *tenderness* and *forever* and *don't go*, flightless
now, swim in circles the lake of drama they only
used to appreciate for what they could see in it
of their own reflections. Too late, of course,
they know better now. They can see the shore,
but cannot reach it. They can see the cattails
that grow thick there, blown to seed, as happens,

yes, necessarily, and just beyond the cattails, rioting
as usual in banks of color, the flowering shrub
called oleander, each part of it poisonous, but most
especially the smoke that, like an unexpected
second bloom, the plant indifferently
releases, when set on fire.

To Autumn

      Whatever it is that, some nights,
can rescue cricket song from
becoming just more of the usual
      white noise—tonight, it's working.
The hours toss with the apparent
weightlessness of leaves when each
      leaf seems, for once, its own dream,
not part of the larger, more general
dream of leaves being limited to tossing
      with either diminishment
or renewal, when why should those
be the only choices? What about joy,
      and despair? What about
ambition?

      •

      If wild, I was once
more gentle. There's a version of
      autumn where the stars' reflections
on the river tonight look, at one moment,
like freight thrown overboard;
      at the next, like signal-lights cast up
through water by a city submerged
where the river's deepest. There's
      another version. Holiness has
no limits, there, only two requirements:
to be hidden; to adore what's hidden.

JOHN SKOYLES

The Letters

1.

Letters written decades ago
arrive in a bundle
from a benevolent ex.

Words I once put
into a young man's mouth
return to mine.

2.

Phrase by phrase, I move my lips
like someone learning to read.

Over time,
the dummy tells the ventriloquist
what to say.

3.

Pounded keys
from an IBM Selectric
have punctured a few pages.

If you lift one to the light,
a constellation appears.

4.

Each signature's etched
as if on the wall of a cell.

The author's gone—released
on time served? Escaped?

Execution is a kind of pardon,
the warden told me
when I taught at Auburn Prison.

5.

I feel a thread unspool
from school to work,

romance to divorce,
from sober to blotto

to black-out and back.

6.

after Transtromer

My house is all skylight and daylight—
panels and transoms
look through to the bay.

One pane's cloudy with a broken seal:
the watermarked page where I'll write my reply.

7.

What tone to take?
A note of thanks?

Remorse
or flirtatious
epistolary horseplay?

Asking these questions
of myself is absurd,
almost insane.

Yet decade after decade,
I've brought my life
to life
in just this way.

8.

The postmarks recall
crossing a bridge

above a dry riverbed
to buy stamps.

The span served no purpose
but continued

over that blunt gorge
as traffic

traded one side
for another,

swapped farewells
for arrivals,

destinations
for just passing through.

9.

There's still a pulse
in these return-to-sender pages.

Their wish to seduce
and secure

came true just half-way.
Blood daubs the flap

where a papercut
sliced a lip or tongue.

She understood
some of what the writer

bled, but not everything.
Should he say it now?

Are years sufficient
to measure time?

Ask the hornet
on the arm

of the white wicker chair
this cold fall day.

His unsteady
struggling tells it all.

DESPY BOUTRIS

These Trees Know Fire the Way My Body Knows Touch

I have always been
        dry grass.   Smoke.
The ruins that make up

                my grandfather's home.
This night, the scent
        of fennel.   The scars
on my wrists and arms.

                        And what is a girl
but a knife. All wilderness. God,
you can't expect me to be

                good.
I'm half-thicket,   half-thorn.
I'm half-made

                of water.
Up ahead there's a barn
                that's on fire. No,
it's covered in autumn leaves. And water floods
from my eyes. No,

                        it's rain, falling
from above. From the clouds
        straining the sky. The trouble
with water:

                it lets nothing go
untouched.   Like hunger.
And what was my crime but to turn to water:
to let nothing go

                        untouched,
tracing a wrist-bone, a bow
        of lips. Fingers tracing the veins
of the leaf I plucked

                off a branch.

Thumbing the blade
        of a butter knife. I watch
the grass bow to the breeze
and I submit
                      to my hungering hands.
To the burning barn within me.

PABLO MEDINA

Canticle of the Mirror

for Kassie Rubico

It isn't in the mirror of today
                    I see myself or yesterday
or back when I lived
                    behind the funeral home
and spied the corpses
                    brought in body bags late at night
or further back when
                    the house cat ate her kittens
and the hurricane blew away
                    the mango tree
it's in the space between time
                    and memory between
the death knell and the river
                    its armature called shadow
tempering the sun
                    and darkening the water.

                    •

My mother once told me she saw God
                    walking around the yard
green and glum
                    like a three-toed sloth
then she sang
                    el negrito tá en la tumba
y naide lo ba bucá
                    ne ne na na ne ne na na
old love old bones
                    the winding mossy way
to the end of self

                    to the dog of solitude
eager to chew on stones
                    have you ever had your fate
withheld and it's the wind
                    tapping your shoulder
telling you it's time
                    el negrito tá en la tumba
a song about a black boy
                    in the grave
ne ne na na ne ne na na
                    not my kind of doom
no one will notice or turn
his way no one torn from her room
                    to seek him out the trees rise
to the iridescent light of night.

                    •

Mirrors speak to one another
                    and multiply
I see myself repeated
                    present to past to moon's milk
dripping out of the sky
                    then the murmur
of what speaks without knowing
                    then the fog spreading
over the pines as spring
                    swallows ambition
and the first insects awaken.

                    •

River high after last night's rain
                    sooner than I want the day will end
and dream be real and real stamp
                    its feet and clamor for the sunset
and the thrush's song
                    (luck turned back at the gate)
sweet long thing sweet long running
                    thing I wish I knew

how love strikes
          like the brain's refrain
back and forth and back again
          river high today after last night's rain.

          •

The art of a blindman looking at the sky
          the art of the equinox of your voice
the art of smiling at the face of death
          the art of digging through the dust and clay
the art of my people the trees
          the art of the stones like the eggs of time
the art of the hill's reprise
          the art of knowing how to close my eyes.

DAVID KIRBY

The Cottingley Fairy Hoax

A jockey who was on a strict diet had a single almond
for dessert, but he was going on a trip, so he took the almond
on the plane with him. I wonder if he ever ate it. Isn't it better
to want something than to have it? In 1917, two young cousins
go down to a stream at the bottom of a garden and take photographs
of fairies which are actually cut-outs which Elsie Wright, age 16,
had copied from a children's book. She and 10-year-old Frances
Griffiths take turns posing with the sprites, then develop
the photographs in Elsie's father's darkroom and show them to
their parents. The father doesn't believe the fairies are real.
The mother does. She brings the pictures to a meeting
of the Theosophical Society, and then all of England sees them,
and then the world. The war had just ended. A grieving public
wanted to believe in an invisible realm that revealed itself
from time to time, and the language used to describe the fairies
shows that: one enthusiast said of the fairies that the girls
were able "to materialise them at a density sufficient
for their images to be recorded," and Arthur Conan Doyle
himself believed that "a visible sign was coming through."
Before long, Elsie and Frances had grown tired of their prank,
but they were embarrassed to say so, and by then it was too late.
In a 1985 interview, Elsie said, "Two village kids and a brilliant
man like Conan Doyle—well, we could only keep quiet."
Frances said millions believed in the fairies because they wanted
to believe, and today, in the dark corners of the internet,
some still do. But the fairies aren't the miracle. The miracle
is that the girls made up the fairies. And that for so long they lied.

JANINE JOSEPH

Near the End of Our Time

she asked me to imagine with her

        that it was as if I'd—and I closed my eyes,

knowing where her sentence

            would twist. My faulting in the year

meant I could draw a shroud and visualize

        —not *nothing*, exactly, but nothing

on or *of*, say, the seaside

            in the relaxation exercise. Upon no meadow,

I had no toes to curl and release

        until the bottoms of my feet were greened

with calm. I'd jerk at the fall

            of no leaf, scatter no pinecones on no amble

along the forest of my systematic imagining.

        Sheep bounding clockwise to bedtime

would subduct at my lids' shutting, my mind's eye

            dilating black as a Blacknose. I couldn't conjure

a tongue, a cheek, my shoulder, an entire

       right arm, a fist to clench in the lapping of breaths. Relax.

Open your mouth wide

            enough to stretch the hinges of your jaw,

read her sheets at home where I gaped

       between sessions, cavernous as a casket.

LAREN McCLUNG

Abyss

Here it is always night. Beyond
ocean ridge & deep sea volcanoes
past the blue & yellow dunes
water thrashes the trenches like music
through convolutions of sleep.
Everything here at least half wakes
toward the surface or drifts down.
The flowers, yes, have mouths
& the rocks, legs. Black swallowers
unhinge their jaws for snake mackerel,
dragonfish flash needle-fine teeth
against their lit-up human skin.
In an instant the seafloor shifts
like synapse, or memory. Coffinfish
& chimaeras bottom-dwell under
the weight of water. Fangtooth,
hagfish & sea spider congregate
where the seafloor begins its descent.
In lucid sleep everything watches
from outside itself, aware
of its own *Dasein* & time pulses
with no measure but the random
lightshow in the eccentric spherical brain
of the octopus swimming head-footed,
gosh, how it sculpts its own likeness
into a cloud of ink, its real skin
a colorful, epicurean symphony
that culminates in a small death,
transcending, melancholy. It remembers
being mollusk, its selfless body
folding toward the anus. For eons
it has been led only by a yearning,
propelled through pitch blackness

uncoiling & following its own light.
Its *Geist* lures an onlooker & yes,
it knows the art of making another fall
in love. Don't wake now though the music
they are making is deafening here.
It has mastered its own desire,
& in the act of touching makes its pearl,
which you'll have to cut out of its body
if you want to hold it in your open hand.
Keep watching how they move
with malice, their eight arms wrestling
before one ultimately loves the other
into oblivion. There is no way to surface,
but lay down on the seabed to recover
your fish from way back in memory.

NIHAL MUBARAK

Ahmed's Story

THE STORY BEGAN TO CIRCULATE at the end of summer, a few weeks after Faisal Babiker's son went missing. As was the case with any new occurrence, it would not be long before everyone heard a different variation of the story. For a while, it would seem as though every person in Khartoum knew about Ahmed Babiker and his sudden disappearance.

•

IT was a dry summer in Khartoum, which meant that people stayed in their homes for as long as they could, willing the electricity to stay on so their air conditioners would continue to work. The stifling heat gave them a reason to call each other and catch up on all the news they had missed, especially the older women. While their husbands and sons went out into the afternoon sun to work, the women booked appointments to have their hands and feet painted with henna and organized tea parties for their neighbors, content to sit at home and gossip until the heat wave passed.

Word traveled fast in the neighborhood of Arkaweet. It was a suburb centrally located in the city, and the neighbors had long since learned never to tell each other anything too important. Still, people talked. They couldn't help themselves. They talked at weddings and funerals, at family dinners, in between classes. It was as though they could not bear to keep any stories to themselves.

The owner of a small convenience store overheard a brief conversation between two middle school boys when they came in to purchase soft drinks and snacks. They weren't from the neighborhood, but he had seen them on occasion at the mosque during Friday sermons.

"I heard Ammo Faisal's son failed out of medical school," said one of the boys.

"No, he didn't fail, he just stopped going to classes. One of my friends is his cousin," said his companion. They spoke as though they were taking part in a competition and needed to come up with the most convincing story, though it did not make any difference to the store owner. He rang them up and tried not to appear surprised by what he heard. Faisal's son was an intelligent young man. Everyone knew this. He had received the top scores in the country on his college-entry exams. They had even interviewed him on television. He told himself that these boys were talking about someone else and dismissed the idea, but when he went home that night, he told his wife what he had heard. It was too good not to share.

"Can you believe Faisal Babiker's son dropped out of school?" he asked while getting ready for bed. His wife sat at her vanity, combing her hair and twisting it into buns on top of her head. She turned to face him, her eyes wide.

"No, that can't be true."

"It is," he said, and in order to keep his dignity, told her that he'd heard the news from the boy's uncle. It would not do for his wife to know the truth, for gossip was a woman's game.

•

"It's such a shame about that boy," Laila Mahmoud told her sister without any preamble. They were in the kitchen making supper. Laila was in her fifties and older than her sister by two decades. Both of them were widows and lived in the same house, having married men who left them nothing except too many children.

"Which boy?" her sister asked.

"Faisal and Manal's kid. The medical student. I heard he failed his classes and is staying at home now."

"His parents spoiled him," the sister said, shaking her head. "The same thing happened with Sarah Abdallah's son. Boys who are too close to their mothers will never get anywhere."

Laila hummed to show her agreement. It was true; Sudani boys were too much trouble. She felt sorry for women who birthed boys and was grateful that her late husband's wish for a son had not been granted. Both women stopped stirring the food they were making and muttered prayers under their breaths, glad that they had been blessed with daughters.

•

KHARTOUM summers were unbearable, and the sun could turn your skin to leather if you weren't careful. Aisha and her best friend Maryam knew this, so at recess they stayed in the shade of the patio instead of playing tag with the rest of their classmates. They watched the Grade Five boys chase the younger girls and shook their heads with the wisdom of girls who know that they are too old for such things. Maryam toyed with Aisha's hair, undoing and redoing the individual braids to amuse herself.

"Do you know who Ahmed Babiker is?" Maryam asked.

"Everyone knows who Ahmed Babiker is. He's been on TV!" Aisha said, rolling her eyes.

"Yeah, well, did you know that he ran away from home?"

"No, he didn't. You made that up." Aisha was the more sensible of the two, while Maryam constantly told the girls in their grade love stories. They were never about her, these stories, but about people they all knew. Maryam's mother said she had a mind for storytelling, like her grandfather. Her father said she was simply a good liar.

"I promise I didn't," Maryam said, tugging one of Aisha's braids. "He wanted to get married to this girl, his college sweetheart, but his parents hated her. So they decided to go away together and get married. Isn't that romantic?"

"Where did they run to?" Aisha asked, intrigued in spite of herself.

"Somewhere in Europe, of course."

"What, like Paris?"

"I don't know, maybe."

•

FAISAL Babiker and his wife Manal had only one son, Ahmed. Faisal, an architect, had designed and built the house in Arkaweet not long after Ahmed's birth; they had lived there for twenty-two years. They were not the type to socialize much with their neighbors, unless a special occasion required their presence. Because they kept their distance, for the most part, and no doubt because they were older, the neighbors did not know what to make of them. Manal, especially, who taught history at the high school, was regarded with unease. The other women did not understand why she would choose to work when her husband had a career.

"It's a good thing she only has a son and no daughters," they said. "What kind of example would she be for a little girl?"

Manal knew that the other women in the neighborhood said these things about her, and she was glad she had never made the mistake of seeing them as friends. While she did not care what anyone said about her, she feared for her son. Her mother had warned her a long time ago that women who spend their time talking behind each other's backs are jealous women, and jealous women have the strongest evil eyes. Manal did not doubt this, for she had seen first-hand what effects the evil eye could have on a person. There had been many women when she was growing up in Kordofan who had lost their children in the womb, whose husbands died young. When she grew older, her mother explained that these women had been the victims of black magic, and she taught her the verses from scripture to recite at night in order to protect herself.

Manal was aware that she no longer held any influence over her son. She had lost that right once he became a man. She could not hold him to her breast and rock him to sleep just to reassure herself, as much as she would have liked to do so. But she was right to worry, because Ahmed was a handsome young man. He had inherited his height and frame from his father, but his facial features were hers. He had eyes that were almost too large for a boy, with thick lashes that fanned over his cheeks whenever he slept. His skin, neither too light nor too dark, never tanned too much in the summer, despite the harsh sun. His hair was soft and curly, so different from his father's coarse strands. He had also taken after her in other ways. He loved to learn, and had proven to his parents from an early age that he would do well in his studies. When he was accepted into the best medical school in Sudan, Manal had been even more proud than her husband. But she knew that these same assets and accomplishments provided the perfect opportunity for the women in the neighborhood to give her son the evil eye, even indirectly. She knew that some of them, the ones with daughters his age or a little younger, would want to claim him, if they hadn't already.

When they found out that Ahmed was missing, Manal would first think of these women. She did not doubt that they were capable of cursing her son's good fortune. She would kneel on her prayer rug for hours, long after Faisal had gone to sleep, and string her prayer beads through her fingers, hoping to ward off any evil that might have entered their home.

•

THE third-year medical students at the University of Medical Sciences and Technology hated their professors, and were not sure why they had chosen to become doctors in the first place. The heat did not help. It made it difficult for them to focus on their classes, and many of them were prepared to walk out of their dreaded observations and never look back. Of course, they had a rather pressing matter on their minds. When the fall semester began, the students returned to find flyers with Ahmed Babiker's face on them taped to the walls outside their classrooms. Those who knew Ahmed personally had already heard of his disappearance, but the younger students were taken aback.

"You mean he just vanished?"

"Are the police looking for him?"

"Maybe he overdosed on something. I heard a lot of the third-year students have been taking sleeping pills," one first-year said to a group of his friends at lunchtime in the canteen. It was true. The workload had gotten to be too much for some of the third and fourth-years. But when they asked for less work, they were told by their teachers that if they couldn't handle medical school, they were welcome to leave like the failures they had proven to be. The students, who felt like failures but did not want to prove their professors right, took pills to help them sleep at night and ones to keep them awake in their classes. Two students had accidentally overdosed the previous semester.

"Are you kidding? Ahmed Babiker, taking pills? Have you even met the guy?" said another first-year, shaking his head.

"Yeah, man, Ahmed is a saint. He wouldn't do anything wrong."

"How do you know?"

"Everybody knows. He never goes to parties, and he spends a lot of time at the masjid when he's not studying. Besides, he's not dead. They would've found a body by now."

"Do you think Dina knows where he is?" This from a second-year girl who did not know Dina personally but had heard of her. Everyone had. She and Ahmed were close friends. They studied together in the library or at the café, and when they weren't studying their families were always at the same gatherings. In fact, they spent so much time together that everyone, even the faculty, assumed the two would get married after graduation.

A group of girls later found Dina sitting in her usual cubicle in the library. They were fifth-year students, ahead of Dina by two years.

"Is Ahmed really gone, or did he just drop out?" they asked her.

Dina said she didn't know. If he had decided to stop going to classes, he hadn't told her about it. The girls didn't believe her.

"But you're his *sweetheart*!" They said, grinning and elbowing each other. "He tells you *everything*. Why would he disappear without telling you first? Or take you with him?"

Dina did not respond. She allowed them to jeer at her until they grew tired of the teasing, rolling their eyes at her back. They were jealous because Ahmed only talked to her. He was the smartest and most good-looking boy in their class, and every girl at the school had envisioned herself as his wife. But none of them compared to Dina. She had fair skin, long, black hair that fell to her waist, and eyes the color of honey. When she was younger, Dina's grandmother told her she was too beautiful to be fully African.

"You have Arab blood in you, my dear," she would say. "Your eyes are too much like the eyes of an Arab princess. And your skin is far too light. And that hair! Now tell me, where on earth did you get hair like that?"

Ahmed had laughed when Dina told him this.

"African women can't be beautiful?" he asked her. "I think your grandmother was just jealous." They had been studying for an anatomy exam under the famed lemon tree in the medical school's courtyard. It was said that the lemon tree had first appeared years ago, long before the university was built. No one could recall the tree growing in stages; it had simply appeared in its full form one morning. This was strange enough, but people noticed that the lemon tree also never shed its leaves. Its branches were always full and green, and it bore its fruit every day of the year. During exam season, the students at UMST sat in the tree's shadow, hoping that its miraculous qualities would transfer to their exam grades.

Ahmed did not believe the story of the miracle tree. He told Dina it was a fairy-tale that students made up because they needed to believe they could do well in their classes. But Dina was a romantic who loved fairy tales, and she told Ahmed that he had too much of a scientific mind. She could only recall those small moments with him, the moments that seemed inconsequential now that he was gone. Dina tried to remember if Ahmed had told her anything in the past that would help his family, anything that would dispel what others were saying about him and his disappearance. It angered her, what she heard the students tell each other, because they didn't know Ahmed like she did. But part of her was beginning to think that even she had not known him at all.

•

WHAT no one knew about Ahmed, even his parents, was that he had decided in his second year of medical school that he did not really want to be a doctor. He discovered a love for poetry and began to attend readings and open mics in the city. While his classmates went out to party and smoke shisha, Ahmed went to cafes in Khartoum to hear people perform on dimly lit platform stages. It gave him a break from reading his textbooks, and soon he began to try his hand at writing poetry himself. He realized that he might be a romantic after all, like Dina, since his poems were often about her. But he did not tell anyone about the poetry. It would disappoint his parents, who expected him to study medicine. Everyone expected him to be a doctor, and he was good at meeting other people's expectations of him. And even though he excelled in his classes and knew that he could be a physician, a good one, he felt that he needed to do something else. He prayed like his mother taught him whenever he needed to decide something and was unsure what to do. "Rely on God," she would say. "He will guide you." Ahmed prayed, and because he loved his parents, he decided to finish medical school, to keep poetry as something he did only occasionally. But he began to pay less attention in his classes, writing poems on the margins of his notebooks instead of taking notes. Still, he continued to do well, and no one noticed any differences in him.

•

THERE were almost as many funeral ceremonies in Khartoum as there were weddings, especially in the summer. People had grown used to it. They would attend afternoon prayers in the mosque and follow a funeral procession to the cemetery, before returning home to prepare for a wedding the same night. There was one such wedding in the neighborhood of Al Amarat, not too far from Arkaweet. The wedding had yet to begin. It was just after ten o'clock and the invitation had said 8:30. This was nothing new. The men claimed that their wives made them late, and the women said that if their husbands bothered to help them get the children ready they wouldn't be late. It was hard to say who was right. Sudani women would be late to the birth of their own child if they could manage it.

Faisal Babiker's brother, who had been asked by Faisal to attend in his place, was standing outside of the function hall when an older gentleman approached him and asked about his nephew.

"The boy is too smart for his own good," Ahmed's uncle, whose name was Samir, said, laughing. He was a large man, and the fabric of his jalabiya stretched over his stomach. "But he is doing well, Uncle, thank you for asking."

Of course, he did not know if this was true. But Faisal and Manal, after hearing some of the stories that were going around about their son, had decided to keep their lips sealed about the whole situation, and their family members were instructed to do the same. They knew people would ask. Of course people would ask. They were like vultures, waiting for someone else's tragedy to occur so they could thank God it wasn't them. There is a saying among grandmothers: A man will murder a person and then attend his funeral. This older gentleman questioning Ahmed's uncle was one such man. He appeared concerned, but in fact he had taken part in adding his own story to the others. He was a faculty member at the University of Khartoum and knew one of Ahmed's professors. The two men had met for coffee the previous day and speculated about the boy's whereabouts. The professor, a balding man in his late sixties, had been sure that Ahmed was involved in something sinister.

"I heard that the boy has been struggling," the older man said now. The air that night was too humid, even for Khartoum. Samir wiped his brow with a cloth handkerchief and flashed his teeth at his companion.

"And who have you heard that from?"

"No one in particular, you just overhear things, sometimes."

"Ah, well, you know what they say about gossip, Uncle."

The older man cleared his throat, looking perhaps a bit disappointed.

•

MANAL sat at her desk. It was the last class of the day. Over the last few weeks, it had been difficult to continue coming in to work and teach other people's children when she did not know the whereabouts of her own child. She wanted to stay at home, but Faisal encouraged her not to, saying that she needed the distraction, and if she stayed home she would only think of Ahmed. He was wrong. She always thought of Ahmed, but at least here she could focus on her students for a few hours. They were in Grade 11, basically adults. Next year they would be in college and Manal would inherit another group. She remembered when Ahmed was in his last year of high school. He had known early on that he wanted to be a doctor and never stopped reminding Manal and Faisal of his future plans.

"Mama," he would say as a child, "I'm going to be a heart doctor. I want to fix people's hearts when they break."

Manal had known that it would not take long for people to hear about Ahmed. She guessed that the story first began to go around at the university, because his classmates would have noticed that her son was not showing up to his classes. For days, their neighbors brought them trays of food and gave their condolences, the women reassuring Manal that Ahmed would return. She knew this show of concern was insincere; they only came to visit because they wanted information. Manal never refused to see them, because she was a gracious host, but she wished that she could close the door in their faces.

His absence was not alarming to them, at first. Ahmed often went on week-long fishing trips with his friends, and they had taken one of these trips before the semester began. But it was strange that he did not tell them he planned to leave, and when she and Faisal received no word from him for seven days, Manal began to worry. She told her husband that their son and the other boys could have gotten stranded on the fishing boat. The rainy season had begun and it made the Nile unpredictable. Faisal, who was a practical man, told his wife that he hoped Ahmed had prepared for the rain ahead of time.

"The boy is book-smart, but I doubt he'll know what to do if they get stuck," he said.

Manal tried not to show that she was afraid in front of Faisal. Her husband thought that worrying about a grown man was foolish. But he did not understand that she was a mother. She worried that their son was in trouble and tried to remember the last thing they had said to one another, but she could not. It must have been something trivial. On the tenth day of her son's disappearance, she took all the old photo albums out from the back of her closet and looked through them when Faisal was at work. She tried to tell herself that Ahmed was still the same boy she saw in the photos, that he had not become someone else. She knew him better than anyone, and if he had changed without her noticing it would devastate her. On her own, Manal decided to look through her son's things, checking his closet and his desk for anything that would help them figure out where he had gone. She found nothing except Ahmed's textbooks and school things, stacked neatly on top of one another, along with the medical supplies he would need that year. The room was organized, and it disturbed her to see how clinical everything looked. The bed was made and the curtains were drawn over the small window, the sun casting shadows onto the bare walls. There were no signs to indicate that someone lived in this space. Manal did not tell her husband about this. She kept her worries to herself and told herself that Ahmed would call.

After two weeks had passed, Faisal began to get angry, saying that the boy could at least give them the courtesy of calling. He made up his mind that their son was going through a late rebellious phase and would be back sooner or later to apologize for having worried them.

It had not occurred to either of them to think of him as missing, not until the other boys returned from the fishing trip without Ahmed, and she and Faisal learned that their son had not gone with them.

·

THE rain was more violent that year than it had been in a long time. It was almost September, and the streets of the city were still flooded with muddy rainwater, forcing people to stay in their homes. Soon, the sandstorms would begin. In Arkaweet, the streets and houses disappeared behind clouds of dirt after a kataha. The wind pushed the sand everywhere, especially in the gaps underneath doors and windows, so that people woke up in the aftermath to find their homes were unrecognizable. After the heavy rains of July and August, which brought temporary relief from the summer heat, these sandstorms were an unwelcome intrusion.

On the last day of the month, Faisal Babiker was returning home from the police station. There had been a storm the night before, and the neighborhood streets were stained yellow. Faisal drove with the windows down so he could see the road. At the station, he had spent an hour talking to an officer who did not look much older than his son, and was told that the department's resources were limited but the police were doing everything they could. When the officer asked him if he knew what Ahmed did outside of school, if he was involved in other activities, Faisal realized that he could not remember the last time he had spoken to his son about anything besides his studies. He did not know if Ahmed still played football with the other neighborhood men on Friday nights, or if he enjoyed any other sport. But the officers said they were referring to anything that might get his son in trouble with the wrong people. Drugs, they said. Weapons. Faisal laughed in their faces. He knew his son would not be involved in anything illegal; the boy was too much like his mother. Still, he felt that he had failed, somehow, as a father. He was ashamed to admit to the officer that he and his son were not close. He knew that the police would take him less seriously now that they were aware of this. Ahmed is a grown man, they would say to each other once Faisal was gone. If he was a child, it would have been a different matter. But he was twenty years old and he could go where he wanted. Besides, his father doesn't even know him. Maybe that's why he left.

Faisal sat in his car once he reached the house and for the first time wondered if it was possible that his son was not coming back.

Two more months passed. Ahmed's parents locked themselves in the house and refused to see anyone. Manal was inconsolable, her pain loud and absolute, but it was her husband's grief that threatened to destroy him. He had taken a leave of absence of work, spending hours on the prayer mat in the living room, his head bowed in a silent show of submission.

Faisal questioned the choices he'd made as a father, especially the way he had raised his son with such coldness and impartiality, as he himself had been raised. While it had never occurred to him that his parenting might have had a negative effect on Ahmed, these choices haunted him now and did not allow him to rest at night. When he prayed, Faisal asked for forgiveness. He began to sleep in Ahmed's room, emerging only to eat meals when his wife insisted that he join her. They ate in the kitchen, having discovered that the dining room was too large for two people, picking at plates of food that neither of them could taste. After weeks of this, during which scarcely a word passed between them, they each wondered, privately, if their sorrow would be enough to kill them.

•

When the rain and sandstorms stopped and it looked like the heat was finally gone, people continued to talk about Ahmed.

"Let's face it, the boy wasn't as smart as his family liked to believe," said a genetics professor, who had not taught Ahmed but felt it necessary to contribute his opinion.

"He probably ran off with a girl and his mother is too ashamed to admit the truth," said Azza, who was a seamstress in Arkaweet.

"I always said that family is strange. They keep to themselves, never talk to anybody. It's not natural. The poor boy probably left because he couldn't stand it any longer." This from Faisal and Manal's next-door neighbor, an old woman named Alawiya. She sat on her bed, knitting a set of doilies for the coffee table. Her daughter, who was not married and lived with her mother, just listened to the old woman, knowing better than to comment.

"It's a shame, really. He would have been such a great son-in-law," Majda Amin told her daughter, who rolled her eyes.

This would go on for some time, until one day the imam's daughter confided in a friend at her cousin's wedding that she was expecting a child. The friend, who was sworn to secrecy, promised the imam's daughter that her secret was safe. A week later, the imam was chased out of the mosque by the congregation. They accused him of not raising his children as a pastor should, of bringing shame to the community. The men in the neighborhood went to the imam's house at night and threw crude torches made from broken tree branches at the windows. The house was empty, for the imam had taken his wife and children and fled to another city, but his neighbors were not aware. The imam would soon learn that his daughter had been assaulted on her way back from class, but the neighbors did not know this. They called her ugly names and cursed her family and their lineage, and when the girl later lost the child they would not know that, either. But it did not matter, because now there was something else to talk about in Arkaweet, and people forgot about Ahmed Babiker.

Translation Folio

CHUS PATO

Translator's Introduction

Erín Moure

CHUS PATO (OURENSE, 1955) IS one of Europe's greatest contemporary poets, and an indispensable force in Galician and Spanish culture. In *Un Libre Favor*, her twelfth book of poetry, Pato acknowledges an unrequitable gift: that of poetry, the language of poetry, the possibility of poetry, and its freedom.

Her Galician title, word by word, means "A Free Favor" and echoes Immanuel Kant's view of aesthetic possibility as freedom: *die freie gunst*. In Galician, *favor* is a gift, a favoring, something bestowed without hope of return. Three Galician words can mean "free": *libre*, from "liberty" and *de balde* or *gratuíto*, "free of charge." In English, "free" is our one adjective, and its mercantile echoes overpower the idea of freedom, leaving too strong an echo of "free of charge." Best to take another title, and Chus Pato gave the nod to *The Face of the Quartzes*.

In *The Face of the Quartzes*, Pato explores our relation as *sapiens* with nativity, the natal, life, its impropriety (that cannot be property), with the natural world, and with language itself, in times that can seem close to an end-time for the planet. Pato cites Friedrich Hölderlin—18th/19th century German philosopher and key figure in German Romanticism—to say that poetry is part of that which we are born to, part of the *natal* of which Hölderlin wrote. Yet, though proper to us, "what we are born to" is not our property; we do not *own* it any more than we own our lives. This is the paradox of art, of life, of poetry. It is a paradox of openness; it is an impropriety both dark and celebratory.

This new book deploys taut and minimalist image-words from architecture, transport, megalithic tombs, animal lives, and mythic figures that are ancient explanations of our human capacity for thinking, speech, muteness. In the poems, the words can give—paradoxically—a sensation of mysticism, but this poetry is material, not mystic. Though they can seem the cry of a sybil, the harbinger of a coming doom (without salvation), they are not; they harken, rather, to *what is*. Readerly reception being grounded in a whole field of cultural references, Pato's referents can't help but shift in the move from Galician to American culture, but they still point to a materiality held in language, transmitted in language, engaged by the human articulated voice. Pato's poems—in this manual for living that is one with birds, with animals, with peaks and trains and lighthouses, and with women poets who undertake boat journeys or cross bridges— show us what it is to inhabit the world of words, of communicative possibility, in the face of aging, and in the face of planetary desolation (on a planet of enduring beauty).

Galicia is a promontory of stone sitting on the Iberian peninsula above Portugal.

Its language, Galician, derived from Latin, is the root language of modern Portuguese and stubbornly survives north of the Miño River. Though long part of Spain, Galicia, with its Celtic substrate and different history and language, has never become simply Spanish. *The Face of the Quartzes* is rooted in the Galician interior city of Ourense, where the poet was born and raised during the long 20th century Spanish dictatorship of Francisco Franco. Ourense was long ago the Roman city of gold (*ouro*) and of dawn's golden light (*aurora*); Galicia may have been at the fringe of the Roman Empire but it was a country of philosophy, and of international travel and influence. Its mountainous rocky interior was mined for gold and iron, metals key to ornament and armament. Its ports were cosmopolitan. Its fishermen were known from the Baltic to Africa to the shores of Newfoundland and Maine. It was a place peripheral and central at the same time. Though today Galicia is even more peripheral in world politics, Chus Pato's poetry recenters it.

In Neolithic times, the Celtic peoples of Galicia would insert white quartz cobbles at intervals among the stones that marked the east face of their megalithic tombs. The eastern wall, facing dawn, marks the portal between the world of the living that of the dead. When sunrise hits its quartzes, the light is extreme. At this moment when the quartz glows, we can pass between the worlds. Both worlds are available. It is a moment and history that engenders the work of art itself. At this portal between the living and the dead that is poetry's gift or favor, Chus Pato writes: *I want to have grey hair/ I want to grow old.* Her book is the cry of life.

Pato is one of the great poets of our time, to me, one of the real risk-takers and thinkers in contemporary poetry. Her poems press on the physical world. They are an ecology: urgent markers of land and beings and relations, markers of freedom in the headlong rush of a contemporaneity that today troubles old views of bodily relations more than ever. Along with Rosalía de Castro, key poet of the Galician nineteenth century, Chus Pato links us through her forms and figures to the "missing people" evoked by Gilles Deleuze, to the "distribution of the sensible" of Jacques Rancière (the new making of art), and to the "volition" and "performativity" articulated in Judith Butler's feminist work on body, precarity, world.

To look outside our own self-image and, instead, into the passage between worlds—the passage that is ultimately human being and that holds the freedom that is art—this is what Chus Pato brings us. Her words in *The Face of the Quartzes* open a reconsideration of freedom, a reconsideration of what we are born to and what forms us, what keeps us in this world, and a consideration of what the world and its history means for women, and for women who write words (who are not always received with openness).

The Face of the Quartzes gives us a portal and a chance to act as humans, *outside the book* now, so that the end-times will not arrive to us, just yet.

After all, I too (and you!) *want to have grey hair / want to grow old.*

CHUS PATO : Four Poems from *The Face of the Quartzes*

Where dream lifts you you're smaller than a flower
notwithstanding that the wind riffles the grasses

where the stone rises over you
you're at the portals of the world
there you extend your hand
there you theorize

on white cinder
on wood bright with light
on the distant ones

as in the nights that are traversed by swimming

at the far reach of the infinite

From the eagle
from one of its wings

bone
for the flute
of the shepherd

the beak sunk in the flesh
devours it

no interjection for astonishment
mouth sealed by five fingers

from one wing
a bone

for music

She loved cities
loved that city

loved the bridges and the vegetation that grows on bridges
loved the wagtails hunting the waters
the deserted thermal pools

loved that city fiercely

loved
above all
loved its woods

the city spun
like the swings of a carrousel
like the meridians
since Genesis

through it
she wore sandals in summer
and sleek canvas sneakers in winter

what remained was
the vertigo that sustains the weight of the rails
and the vagabonds who register the impossible humidity of the ether

in a way not dissimilar to how the arch extends outward
and the sea cormorant unfurls over raw icepans

in blizzards

in the amplitude of the world

the train passes
over the waters

We were upon some peak
like models for a painter of the Quattrocento

at the tunnel
the trees were with me

the bus
that on the canvas couldn't quite make the turn
beam of headlights that split the night
and sheared us
that part of the mind in which a person can remain alone
perpetual

some time ago
reached destination

translated from the Galician by Erín Moure

VICTORIA CHANG

Dear Mother,

I found a box with some of your papers. Inside that box was your marriage license. I know so many things now. I know you were 24 and father was 26. I know father was a project engineer at General Motors and you were a research assistant in the physics department at the University of Michigan. I know that the physics gene did not pass down to me. I know you went to the county to get married.

I know your parents' names: Shih-Tou Chang and Phon-Mei Lee; Pao-Lan Jin and Gee-In Chang. I know the name of your father, Pao-Lan Jin. I know your mother was also a Chang.

I wonder about your witnesses? I wonder where they are now? Wen-Jei Young and She-Zuan Zang. They both lived at 2214 Yorktown Drive in Ann Arbor, Michigan. Were they roommates? Were they married? I can't even tell if these are men or women. I've never known if you can tell gender in a Chinese name. I never thought to ask before and now it's too late.

I wonder where the two county clerks are now—Luella M. Smith and Carol A. Miller. This language slips right off my tongue. I know both of them are women. I know that Smith and Miller are common American names.

I know the year is 1966, three years before my sister would be born and four years before I would be born. I can't read the marriage judge's name but I think it is a man's name. I know it's cursive and I can read and write cursive. I wonder what he thought when four Chinese people came into his court? I wonder if he felt a kind of prickling on his face. I wonder whether he was happy for them.

I imagine you sweating under your nice dress. I imagine it being a pastel blue. I imagine the horizon that day bending towards the countries you left. I imagine you were relieved. I imagine you felt wild. I imagine you were scared.

I wonder why you never spoke of this day. I wonder how much of this day was about being practical. I imagine how much of this day was about love. You had come to this country on your own. Who would marry you? Probably not an American. How would you find a Chinese man? How would you survive here by yourself? With no language? No money? Only secrets. You can't buy anything with secrets.

Father lived at 1021 Church Street in Ann Arbor. Google maps brings up a little red house the color of a blush I might wipe on my face. I wonder how many Chinese people lived there. I wonder if you ever stood on the lovely porch. I wonder, when you came down the steps, whether you turned right or left? I wonder if that house was red in 1966. Or if they painted it red because you were Chinese.

You lived on 825 East University Street in Ann Arbor. Google maps brings up a dilapidated yellow house with a gabled roof. In 2015-2016, the *entire building underwent wall-to-wall renovations?* I now know that you lived *just walking distance to the Business School* (according to Redfin).

I wonder why you never told me you lived in Ann Arbor, that you worked at the University of Michigan. Even when I went there myself, you never said a word. I wonder why you told me so little about everything. Or maybe I wasn't listening.

I wonder whether memory is different for immigrants, for people who leave so much behind. Memory isn't something that blooms but something that bleeds internally. Memory is just another thing that disappears because it isn't useful. Not money, a car, a diploma, a job. I wonder if memory for you is a color.

I imagine another kind of mother, an American mother, who might have walked me to 825 East University Street, arm in arm, finger pointing at the pigeon on the roof of the building.

Just two weeks ago, apartment #3 was for rent, the one on the second floor. I wonder what floor you lived on. I wonder whether you had a nice view. I wonder if you had other Chinese roommates. I wonder what you made for dinner each night. I wonder so hard, I can smell the rice cooker and hear the steam.

Google maps tells me you lived two minutes from each other. I imagine Father visiting you, walking up Church Street, taking a left on Oakland Avenue, and then another right on East University. I imagine you walking down the stairs, no, flying down the stairs to open the door for him. Your heart in your throat by the time you reached the bottom. I imagine your cheeks tacked with desire.

I look on Google maps to see if there's a ghost of you somewhere, of you leaping, of your dress lifting open. And in this moment, your imagined happiness covers my grief like an eyelid.

Dear Mother,

What city were you born in? What was your American birthday? What was your Chinese birthday? It's too late now. But I would like to know.

I would like to know why your mother took you and your six siblings across China to Taiwan with Chiang Kai Shek. I would like to know if you had pockets in your dress. If you wore pants. If your hand held a small stone. I would like to know if you thought the trees were black or green at night, if it was cold enough to see your breath. I would like to know who you spoke to along the way. I would like to know if you had some of those small salty plums we both love in your pocket.

I would like to know if you carried a bag. If you had a book in your bag. I would like to know where you got your food for the trip. I would like to know what your father's voice sounded like. If it was brittle or if it was pale. If it was blue or red.

I would like to know if your mother was afraid. I spent a few weeks with her in Taiwan. She bought me *bao zi* every morning. Do you remember I called you to tell you about the *bao zi* and sweet *dou jiang?* Always too hot for me to drink. She complained to me every morning all summer long. Do you think she loved me for just one summer or was she using me?

She complained of being sick and said my aunt wouldn't help her. How long did it take me to figure out how to call an ambulance? And then when they came, she refused to go. In that moment, I knew you were her daughter. And I was her granddaughter.

Listen. Do you hear that? It's the wind. That's the same wind from your countries. Sometimes if I listen closely at night, I can hear you approach and drop a small bag at the door. When I open the door though, there is nothing there. Just the same wind. Thousands of years old. Happy birthday wind! Happy birthday mother. April 6, 1940. I know this now. All the nurses, doctors, funeral home people, mortician, asked me so I memorized it. Your American birthday, *April 6, 1940,* I said again and again. As if I had known this my whole life.

Dear Sister,

Do you remember that email I sent you about hair pulling? I had typed into Google *hair pulling* and one word stood out: *trichotillomania* or *trich* for short. I'm not sure what led me to type those words or why it took me so long to do so, but I remember spending the next hour reading. That night I dreamt of hair, thousands of small bits falling on me like a confession.

Email allowed me to speak with you without ever having to talk to you. *Have you heard of this?* I typed and sent some links. What happened next surprised me. A long email came back that said: *Yes! I have!* My body shook when you told me this and I couldn't figure out if I was the boat or the person drowning. We never talked about it again.

It's not that we grew up amongst whispers. Loud language was everywhere, bundles of Mandarin from my mother's mouth, mixed with my father's nearly perfect English, but Taiwanese-accented Mandarin. Then our bits of Chinese mixed with English. But your hair was the silence inside of a tree trunk.

I remember the blue boxes arriving in the mail, Chinese characters on them. Mother pouring the brown powder out of each box into Ziploc bags and labeling them with Chinese characters on masking tape. You were supposed to eat this powder and your hair would magically regrow. I wanted to taste the powder. I wanted the powder to grow words.

Silence arranged itself like furniture. I was always bumping into it. When unrelated aunties and uncles came over for dinner parties, did you envy the laughing like I did, the talking that sounded like wind from a different country? They drank Riunite wine over steaming fish and tofu. When they all left, they took these words, left something burned.

I didn't know what was wrong, so I prayed each night to God but God just gave me tomorrow. Eventually, I stopped praying because I realized that God didn't speak the same language as me.

While I sat in my room and imagined stories in my head, you read books. Little strands of hair with droplet-shaped roots stuck to everything. I wondered if the hairs missed your head. I wondered why the hairs refused to hold on.

I remember one summer we drove to some other small Michigan town, maybe Rochester, maybe Birmingham, maybe Troy. Narrow roads and bald trees. Do you remember the faceless foam mannequins covered with wigs? How mother was at the back of the store talking to the woman who tended the register. How you and I wandered the rows. My favorite was the blue one on the empty face with no mouth.

After that, you always wore a black wig. The top of your head beneath it was short black stubbles on the top and some longer strands down the sides of your head in a bob.

Each morning, you put the wig on and attached it with black bobby pins, one by one. I passed by the bathroom quickly as a servant might appear and pick up a glass and then disappear.

Before mother died and before father had a stroke, I tried to tell them that your hair didn't fall out, that you had been pulling it out all along. The air conditioning came on and I ended up nearly yelling. *No,* father said. *I don't think so.* I repeated that I knew for a fact and that you had told me. *No, you're wrong,* he said again. Mother didn't say a word.

Before mother died, I tried one more time. Mother sat in a blue chair with a plastic tube in her nose. *Well,* she said, between the oxygen machine sound that came every few seconds. I sat 10 feet away on a sturdy wooden stool that I now use every day to put on my shoes.

I know mother died knowing you had trich but she didn't need to announce it like I did. Because she didn't need to be better than you.

Dear Claudia,

You call me all the time, as if I am a small bowl of water and you a bird. The problem is that the bowl of water is always empty.

Thank you Claudia for caring for my father. Thank you Claudia for calling me every week. Yesterday you called and I realized you hadn't been calling to give me reports, but to *talk*. I see now you call to tell me about your suffering.

A few days before my mother died, she said: *I'm done. I don't care about him anymore. I'm too tired*. She pressed the button and crossed the street when the blinking man was still red. In some small way, she chose to die so she wouldn't have to care for my father anymore.

Dear Claudia, what if I can't find anyone to take care of my father?

The last time we took my father out to eat was the last time he would ever go out to eat. When we paused in front of a golf course, I looked in the rear-view mirror to see if he had noticed it. His head turned slightly to the right. When we stopped, he looked at the white carts moving, the little men with their sticks pushing dimpled balls around.

I wondered if my father had even a flash of his obsession with golf. He had taped photos of golf swings all over his walls. He had played almost every day for 10 years until his stroke. When we played together, I was at my happiest.

As we passed the golf course, nothing in his expression changed. And I knew then that his brain had become unskeined.

I'm sorry Claudia. I put my father on Seroquel today. My mother would never have done that.

Some days, I want to tell everyone I meet that my mother died. Sometimes I do tell them, just to see who reacts.

I don't blame anyone for not reacting, for most people still live in a bright room. *A bright hour,* as Emerson says. We often say night *falls*. I think the night rises. I think the bright falls.

Translation Folio

RODOLFO WALSH

Translator's Introduction

Cindy Schuster

REVERED IN ARGENTINA AS A brilliant author who exemplified the ideal of the politically committed intellectual, Rodolfo Walsh (1927-1977) is widely recognized as one of the foremost Argentinean writers of the second half of the twentieth century. The descendant of Irish immigrants, Walsh was born in the provincial town of Choele Choel, in northern Patagonia. At the age of ten, with his family facing financial ruin, he was sent to study in the Fahy Institute, an austere Catholic boarding school for impoverished children and orphans of Irish descent, an experience that would later find its way into his fiction. As a young man, Walsh began his writing career as a proofreader, translator, journalist, and editor of anthologies. He soon began publishing detective fiction in magazines, and his first collection, *Variations in Red (1953)*, won a national contest whose judges included Jorge Luis Borges.

In June of 1956, during a rebellion against the military government that had deposed Juan Perón the previous year, the Buenos Aires police rounded up a group of men they suspected of involvement in the uprising and drove them to the outskirts of town, where they were shot and left for dead. Six months later, Walsh was tipped off that one of the executed men was alive. This information spurred him to carry out an exhaustive clandestine investigation, in which he managed to locate and interview the survivors, and collect evidence exposing the crime. The events are reconstructed in *Operation Massacre* (1957), which ushered in the modern genre of testimonial or non-fiction narrative, anticipating Truman Capote's *In Cold Blood* by nine years.

While *Operation Massacre* was the first text to erase the conventional boundaries between fiction and journalism, Walsh's technical and stylistic innovations extend beyond his groundbreaking non-fiction narratives; he is also renowned as a fiction writer, journalist, playwright, and translator of such authors as H. G. Wells, Raymond Chandler, Dalton Trumbo, Jack London, and D. H. Lawrence. From his early works in the tradition of classic British detective stories, his highly literary, stylistically and formally experimental fiction evolved in the 60's and 70's to take on themes of political intrigue, resistance to authority, class conflict, and social marginalization during the historical upheavals of mid-twentieth century Argentina.

"The Traitor's Eyes" is one of Walsh's earlier narratives, and one of his rare forays into the realm of the fantastic. The story takes place in Budapest in 1945, at the end of the Second World War, during the Russian occupation. A Hungarian ophthalmologist, now in exile, recounts the eerie tale of an ill-fated corneal transplant, in which a patient who has been blind since birth receives the eyes of a prisoner condemned to death. The patient's sight is restored, but he is haunted by a strange and disturbing dream that materializes before him each night in greater detail. The terrifying image revealed in the dream leads him to fear for his sanity.

Published in 1952 in the magazine *Vea y Lea*, "The Traitor's Eyes" is marked by the influence of Borges; indeed, Walsh is considered to be one of his literary heirs. Borgesian themes such as the alternate planes of reality, duality, the manifestation of dreams, and the persistence of memory are woven into this story. Like Borges, Walsh's style is elliptical, displaying a meticulous and concise economy of language. And like Borges, his leap into the fantastic is anchored in a richly detailed and specific verisimilitude.

The collection *Worldly Offices* (1965), contains what is undoubtedly Walsh's most well-known story and the first to fictionalize the iconic figure of Eva Perón. "That Woman" alludes to a bizarre historical incident: the disappearance of Evita's corpse after Juan Perón was deposed from power in 1955. The story is written as a dialogue, or verbal contest, between the military official responsible for the kidnapping and a journalist investigating the disappearance. Based on an actual interview conducted by Walsh, the story dramatizes an event omitted from the "official history" of the time, displacing the act of investigation from the realm of journalism onto fiction, during a period when government censorship would have made it impossible to publish such an account in the newspaper.

In 1959, Walsh travelled to Cuba, where he participated in founding the news agency *Prensa Latina*, working closely with Gabriel García Márquez and the Argentinian journalist Jorge Masetti. And it was on a subsequent trip to Cuba in 1961, that Walsh, an amateur cryptographer, managed to decode a CIA telex regarding the Bay of Pigs invasion, forewarning the Cuban government of the impending attack.

Walsh's political activism led him to join the left-wing urban guerrilla group Montoneros in the 1970s, where he worked as an intelligence officer. In 1976 he created the clandestine news agency ANCLA, which circulated news bulletins about the terror unleashed by the junta: kidnappings, imprisonment, torture, death squads. Walsh's daughter María Victoria, also a Montoneros militant, died that year in a shoot-out with military forces.

One year later, on the first anniversary of the coup, Walsh wrote his acclaimed "Open Letter from a Writer to the Military Junta," an eloquent and passionate denunciation of the crimes of the dictatorship. Shortly after mailing copies of the letter to various press agencies, Walsh was ambushed and assassinated by soldiers from the Navy School of Mechanics, which operated as a clandestine detention, torture, and extermination center under the junta. He was 50 years old. His body was never recovered.

RODOLFO WALSH : A Story

The Traitor's Eyes

ON FEBRUARY 16, 1945, RUSSIAN troops completed their occupation of Budapest. On the 18th I was arrested. On the 20th they released me and I returned to my duties in the Department of Ophthalmology at the Central Hospital. I have never known the reason for my detention. Nor do I know why I was released.

Two months later I held in my hands a formal request signed by Alajos Endrey, a condemned man awaiting his execution. He offered to donate his eyes to the Institute for Sight Restoration, founded by me at the beginning of the war, and in which I performed—though it is now denied by Istvan Vezer and the cabal of upstarts who have maligned me and forced me into exile—eighteen corneal grafts in blind patients. Of these, sixteen were a complete success. Patient number seventeen stubbornly refused to regain his sight, even though the operation was technically perfect.*

Case number eighteen is the subject of this account, which I am writing to pass the time in my solitary exile, thousands of miles from my native Hungary.

I went to see Endrey. He was in a small, clean cell, which he paced incessantly, like a caged beast. He did not exhibit a single noteworthy characteristic that would bring him to the attention of a man of science. He was a small, irritable individual, with a look of relentless persecution in his eyes. He presented obvious signs of malnutrition. A brief examination revealed that his cornea was in good condition. I informed him that his offer was accepted. I did not investigate his motives. I knew them full well: last-minute sentimentality, perhaps a dark desire to persist, even if only in a small way, incorporated into the life of another man. I walked off through the gray stone corridors, flanked by the indifferent or hostile gaze of the guard.

The execution took place on September 20, 1945. I vaguely remember a procession of silent, half-asleep men, a dusty path that rose through the brush, an inconsequential dawn. I improvised a surgical table in a hut with a zinc roof, fifty steps from the site of the execution. I thought, idly, that the executed man could have been me, that fate was an absurdity, death a trivial convention.

I prepped the patient carefully. He was blind from birth, due to a cone-shaped deformation of the cornea, and his name was Josef Pongracz. I stitched the sutures through his eyelids to keep them open. It was during this procedure that the fatal shot caught me by surprise.

---

* I believe that in that case the psychological factor was decisive. The patient can in fact see, but he will not acknowledge it, because he is afraid to see, because he does not want to see, because he is accustomed to not seeing. There is no other explanation.

Two soldiers brought the dead man on a handbarrow. A quadruple star of blood decorated his chest. His pupils were dilated in a look of vague astonishment.

I extracted the eye and cut out the piece of the cornea intended for the graft. Then I extracted the damaged area of the patient's cornea and replaced it with the graft.

Ten days later I removed the bandages. Josef sat up and took a couple of hesitant steps. I observed his reactions. His face took on an expression of unspeakable fear. *He saw.* He was lost.

He looked around, searching for me among the objects that constituted the operating room. When I spoke to him, he recognized me; he tried to smile. I told him to go to the window. He faltered, so I took his arm and guided him, as if he were a child. When I put him in front of the window, he closed his eyes, and touched the sill, the frame, the glass panes, over and over again. Then he opened his eyes and looked off in the distance.

"It's getting dark," he said, and began to cry silently.

Two months later I received a visit from Dr. Vendel Groesz, of the Psychiatric Institute. Josef had gone to see him. He found himself, according to Groesz, in a terrible state, a deep mental depression, exacerbated by nightmares and hallucinations; he was at risk of schizophrenia.

Two days after the operation (Dr. Groesz told me) Josef had dreamt about a nebulous panorama, nearly devoid of details: a hill, a path, a gray, spectral light. The dream had recurred seven nights in a row. Despite the innocuous nature of those images, Josef had always awakened in the grip of a dark and unjustifiable terror.

Dr. Groesz consulted his notes.

"It was as if I had been there before, and something terrible was about to happen." Those were his exact words.

Dr. Groesz admitted that in this case all the usual procedures had failed. Whatever Josef's complexes were, they could not be associated with visual sensations or memories, because he had been blind since birth. Since recovering his sight, he had not left the city. So he didn't know, strictly speaking, what a hill was, or a dusty mountain path, unless one could call the imprecise, dimensionless concept, typical of the blind, knowledge. The panorama that unsettled Josef's dreams, was not, then, a visual memory; neither was it a visual memory modified by his particular oneiric symbology, but rather an inexplicable, arbitrary product of his subconscious.

"Dreams," said Dr. Groesz, "as distant as they seem from experience, are always based on it. Where there is no previous experience, there can be no dreams that correspond to that experience. That is why the blind do not dream, or at least their dreams are not constituted of visual representations, but of tactile or auditory ones."

In this case, nevertheless, there was a dream of visual character (whose recurrence indicated its importance), that preceded any visual experience of the same order.

Obliged to seek an explanation, Dr. Groesz had turned to the archetypes or primordial images of Jung—whose theories he rejected as fantasy—a type of oneiric inheritance we receive from our ancestors, and which can burst forth inopportunely in our dreams and even in our conscious life.

"I am a man of science," clarified Dr. Groesz, unnecessarily, "but I cannot disregard any working hypothesis, no matter how contrary it is to my experience and my particular manner of seeing things. But I also had to discard that hypothesis. You will soon see why.

"A week later, the stark, bare panorama of the first dreams began to acquire distinct features, like a slowly developing photograph. One night it was a stone of a particular shape; the next night, a shack with a zinc roof, under the shelter of two identical, barren trees; then a sunless dawn; a dog wandering between the trees . . . Night after night, detail by detail, the scene comes into focus. He has gone so far as to describe to me, in half an hour of exhaustive exposition, the exact shape of a tree, the exact shape of some of the branches of that tree, and even the shape of some of its leaves. The scene is perfected every time. Not a single previous detail is missing. I have proven it. Every day I make him repeat the dream of the night before. It is always the same, exactly the same, *but in more detail.*

"A week ago he mentioned for the first time five figures who had appeared in the scene. Five outlines, five dark forms, silhouetted against the leaden dawn. Four of them are standing abreast, facing him; the fifth, off to one side, is in profile. The following night the figures were in uniform; the figure on the side was wielding a sword. At first the faces were indistinct, almost nonexistent; then they slowly became more defined."

Dr. Groesz consulted his notes once again.

"The figure on the side, wielding the sword, is a young, blond officer. The first soldier on the left is short and fat, and his uniform is too small for him. The second one reminds—notice that he says *reminds*—him of his younger brother; *Josef told me, almost in tears, that he has no brothers, he never did, but that soldier reminds him of his younger brother.* The third has a black moustache and his uniform is very shabby; he avoids looking at him; he looks off to one side . . . The fourth is an enormous man, with a scar across the left side of his face, from his ear to the corner of his mouth, like a winding violet river; a pack of cigarettes sticks out of the pocket of his battle jacket."

Dr. Groesz took a handkerchief from his pocket and wiped his brow.

"Yesterday," he said—and from the way he said "yesterday" I understood that something terrible was coming—*"yesterday Josef saw the scene in its entirety!* My God! My God!

"The soldiers had rifles and they were aiming at him, with their fingers on the trigger, ready to open fire.

"We hospitalized him immediately. He resists sleep, because he is afraid of dreaming that he is before a firing squad, he is afraid to feel that sudden and unimaginable horror of death. But the scene, which before only appeared in dreams, now also haunts him when he is awake. It is enough for him to close his eyes, even in the fleeting moment of a blink, to see it: the officer with the unsheathed sword, the line of four soldiers in firing position, the four rifles aimed at his heart.

"This morning he spoke a strange name. I asked him who it was, and *he said that it was him.* He believes he is someone else. An obvious case of schizophrenia."

"What is that name?" I asked.

"Alajos Endrey," replied Dr. Groesz.

THROUGH the intervention of a military commander—whose name, for obvious reasons, I cannot mention—I was able to interview the officer who conducted the execution of Alajos Endrey. He did not remember me. I, for my part, had barely glanced at him in our previous brief encounter. He consented, with frosty military courtesy, to my preposterous request.

A couple of minutes later, the four soldiers who had composed the firing squad that gray and almost forgotten morning lined up before me. *Then I saw the picture that the ill-fated Josef had seen with the eyes of the traitor Alajos Endrey:*

The first soldier on the left was short and fat, and his uniform was too small for him; in the second I thought I perceived a vague resemblance to Endrey himself; the third had a black moustache and eyes that avoided looking straight ahead; his uniform was very worn. The fourth was an enormous man, with a scar that crossed the left side of his face, like a winding, violet river . . .

translated from the Spanish by Cindy Schuster

MAXINE SCATES

Mirror

Yesterday I threw away a photo of a street where
people I did not know were walking early in the last

century. Yet I kept the photo of the Coca Cola billboard,
lake in the background. In it I saw the world changing,

my world, as in any world we think we know. I kept
the photo of the bomber pilot, a cousin once removed,

who died somewhere over Europe before my time,
and thought of the plane drifting slowly over the spires

and canals of Venice as we came in for a landing. In my
American way, I saw Disneyland below, a brittle

fantasy where swarms of people moved from one
attraction to the next. Years earlier, we'd arrived by train

and joined the crowd in which we could not see
ourselves as we moved slowly out of the station onto

the dock, the Grand Canal opening before us. I guess
it's all a matter of perspective, the way our narratives

tell us the survivors will stagger across the burning
landscape once so endlessly abundant, or, if not burning,

the streets deserted, the window shade still knocking
an empty Coke bottle against a telegraph key as it did

in *On The Beach* when that strange code called to others
who came and found no one was left. But don't

we believe we'll always return? After all, the gods said
they could not imagine earth without us—

which is reassuring, until we remember we are
the ones who imagined them.

YUSEF KOMUNYAKAA

What Kind of Man Am I?

I have held myself responsible
for bitterness in hard crabapples
& other green fruits hastily plucked
near virgin woods, for the howling
wolves encircling a crippled calf
at the edge of a boxwood grove
where an old house has sunken,
for pulling a punch when I knew
I was right, holding my tongue
till a seam grew in heartwood,
for hitting a rich wife-beater
before they both came at me,
for not saying at that perfect
moment, Dear, you're April
in Paris, for laughing when I
wanted to cry, for knowing,
for knowing the taste of clay
red under my skin, for being
unable to back off from blood
on the leaves, running fingers
over the bittersweet evidence,
for all the unspeakable crimes
against shadows of me, myself.

Hemiplegia

A big guy across the rehab
hall, fear & laughter under
his voice, praying for hours,
thunder still in his balding skull,
look-alike for a famous
opera tenor, asking for ice cream,
he can hum a devastating blues,
but needs to calm himself,
to stop talking Hegel & cooing
that word. I think he's saying,
Hamilcar. I don't know about you,
but it's German to me,
& when he says, Move,
now, mother-
fucker, you can
bet your soul
he's scolding
his right hand.

MAUREEN SEATON

In Which the Big C Devours My Spine and Creates a Cockeyed Ladder with One Rung Missing

Sometimes a broken spine feels like the word caterwaul, although there are no cats around to defend themselves.

Specifically, my L3 sports a shadowy grin surrounded by sword-poking Musketeers.

I'm here in Colorado. There are the mountains. There's Buddha in the backyard surrounded by crab apples falling like bombs on his head.

(No worries. Buddha exists beyond his body.)

I will call my upcoming surgery "Psycho-plasty."

Psychoplasty: the injection of cement into a fractured vertebra with the intention of mak-ing the bone immortal.

Immortality was Chioma's idea. I give her complete credit. "Oh, Maureen," she said, "They're making you immortal."

Meanwhile, my doctors sound like this: blah blah plasty, blah blah plasty, blah blah plasty.

I hear: silly putty, boo boo kitty, blah blah nasty.

I will rise from the operating table like Super Glue Girl and fly into the Rockies and skate on the glaciers and slide down the faces of metamorphic rock.

Or: A mountain will come to dwell inside me. It will replace my sorry bones and save my life. My body will be a billion years old.

JP GRASSER

You Call with the Diagnosis

Remember the mare
Mama? Out by the windmill,
foaling? Nothing more

you could do, but still,
you fought. Remember the way
you held her? *Be still,*

you said. The soft gray
of her coat was dark with sweat.
Remember? A ray

lanced the clouds. The wheat
filled its head with easy light.
Remember, you whet

her faint appetite
with an apple slice, then gave
her placenta, bite

by bite. She was saved.
Which am I? Who can be brave?

DAN ALBERGOTTI

The Servant's Ear

> While all four gospels report that one of the disciples took a sword and cut off the ear of one of the arresting priests' servants in Gethsemane, only Luke tells of Jesus replacing the severed ear onto the servant's head.

The servant's ear has fallen to the ground
and hears now, from its nest of bloody grass,
the squabbling of the savior and his men.

And hears, of course, the screaming from the head
that was its home just two seconds ago
and orders hissed by the arresting priest,

then rustling of a processional gait—
the march to make the prisoner face the law—
and silver pieces jingling in a sack.

The footsteps fade. There's not another sound
for hours as history begins to pass
one simple, severed organ without sin.

It will lie for decades on its green bed,
listening to crickets, the occasional crow.
Out of the story, it still has at least

a half a century, maybe more, to wait
for Luke to lift it into myth, to draw
it up and, with his pen, to put it back.

RYAN HABERMEYER

After the End of Color

THE COLOR LIBRARIAN COMES OUT at night because that is when it is easiest to collect the color. He moves slowly but deliberately past houses teeming with ivy, pinching a bit of violet from a crack in the sidewalk and fisting a handful of orange off a mailbox. It used to take less than an hour to fill the bucket, back when a menace of color blanketed the city, but now he is lucky to fill half the bucket on any given night. It is hard to say whether he is good at his job because not even the color librarian is sure what his job is. He tries not to think about it. He tries not to think about the broken windows or rusted bicycles or wonder why he wears a watch but never thinks about time. He tries not to think about the pointlessness of his days and the exhaustion of his nights or the paradox of light—how sometimes it bends and other times reflects, or how light always seems to know where it's going, always stretching, always searching for clean blank spaces. Most of all, he tries not to take his eyes off the road and glance up at the rainbow and its brittle band of light, sad that he will not live long enough to understand the language of color.

THE rainbow came on a Wednesday. A few children spent the afternoon pretending it was a stairwell to a lost kingdom and climbed trees trying to reach it. A week passed before anyone in the city realized it wasn't a normal rainbow, refusing to leave the skyline, stubbornly stretched in the same arc. By the end of the month crowds gathered frequently to watch it, perched like gulls, unblinking. Its colors seemed to intensify. The bands thickened, flickering gently at the edges.

It was a popular attraction. Families gathered at the park with picnic baskets and binoculars. There was music, dancing. Vendors sold brightly colored food. This upset the roller skating rink and movie theatre owners because how could they compete with a rainbow? Florists saw their business triple. People wanted to believe in the rainbow. It could not just be light bending around raindrops, they thought. It must be something else, something more. A dream plucked from a nightmare. For the skeptics a new physics, for the believers the hand of God. People in hot air balloons and hang gliders tried to float through the rainbow. Others stared at it from below, curved in the sky like a hot blind scar.

THE color librarian pauses on the lighthouse. Halfway up the stairwell he offers a rat a bite of cheese. Like most of the city the lighthouse is smeared in grime, in moss, in mold. Just looking at it makes his bones ache and hands cramp. He used to come here with his wife to catch fireflies. Before the blackouts, before the rationing, she would have a dozen jars full of them in the nursery. The color librarian always thought the fireflies were hideous, but he couldn't take his eyes off them. I like to think they're praying, his wife would say.

LESS than a year after the rainbow's arrival it started shedding. Millions of flakes an hour, coating the town in a strange dust. A panel of scientists from the Observatory stood on the gymnasium stage and pointed to charts and spoke about radiational cooling in the lower troposphere bending light at a slower rate which makes rainbows defy the laws of classical mechanics.

What risk does the rainbow pose for children? people wanted to know. Nature does not take risks, the Observatory said. At what point is it not just a rainbow but a sign of something else? A rainbow is not a sign, it can only be a rainbow, the Observatory said. Other questions went unanswered. When will it do something? Can we weaponize it for world peace? Can we nominate it for mayor? What happens if someone touches the rainbow? Is there such a thing as refracted light infection?

It is a sign from God, someone said.

It's science, someone interrupted.

There is no exact science except for God, said another.

THE color librarian is not sure if God put the rainbow in the sky or if science is coming unhinged. Having seen inside the human body, the color librarian used to believe God was a clockmaker with a sense of humor to build a machine like us, and even now he would like to imagine a patient God who leaves blank spaces in the canvas for humans to fill in, but after the bombs, the suicides, the evacuations, the sewers, now that he is alone with the quiet that is both beautiful and frightening, such belief leaves the color librarian with more questions than answers. He does not know if he is lucky, or immune, or being punished, or maybe he is a fairy godfather gathering up the dust of some botched spell.

Is it finished? his wife asked that evening, as if in a trance. He had stayed off the main road coming back from the lake, soaked to the waist, glancing over his shoulder. Already she was throwing things into the fire: towels, pacifier, shoes, blankets. All infected, she said. Removing his wet clothes she added them to the fire. It hissed. Not the pillow, he said, his hands still trembling. Later, after she was gone, he would board up the windows and sit in the room with the empty crib until it was quiet.

It was no use telling her she didn't have to go. He knew there were distances between them. She believed she'd seen the face of god in the sewers. The ark, they called it. He told her to wait up here a little longer. Things might change. Things have already changed, she said. Won't it make you sad to stay here with all this color? she asked from the doorway. Hugging the pillow to his chest he told her, I am always sad.

THE color librarian carefully scoops dust off the lighthouse. Later, he'll sort the color into jars in the library basement. Oranges, reds, blues. Color is strange. Most of the time it is dusty. Occasionally stringy. Sometimes like grains of sand. Each hue has its own personality. He is not sure what they will do with this library of color in the future. Maybe it will save them. Maybe it will tell them how to stop this from happening again. Maybe they will do nothing at all. Indifference is a pleasant disease, killing slowly and kindly. He likes to stare at the jars in the darkness of the library basement, the dust glowing faintly like some new bible written in a language he can't quite translate but maybe someday someone will. He wonders about the alphabet of rainbows. He wonders about words like ecstasy, shame, indifference, penance. He wonders how many buckets it will take until he can shed his memory.

He winds his way back downtown through streets cleaning bridges, cafés, belfries. He avoids the fountain with its sculpted cherubs, afraid of the ghostly reflections of the drowned lurking in the water. What matters after the end of color, he thinks, is to keep moving. Light bends into a hundred colors, but somehow time has only a single arc. The color librarian thinks this is cruel but just.

He saves the church for last. He cleans the pulpit, the pews, the altar. He spends more time than he should making sure the little pillow where believers use to kneel has all the dust shaken from it.

One night he found god hiding in the sacristy, an old man with glazed, red-rimmed eyes. He sat next to the old man and picked the nits from his beard. You can come with us, the god said, you can come home. It's not finished, the color librarian said as if in a trance. He reached into his pocket to share some cheese with the god but when he turned back there was only a rat.

The color librarian stares at the rainbow through the collapsed roof. Tonight it seems pale, like a bent skeleton of light. It must be lonely up there. The color librarian scratches his beard. It's lonely down here too.

THE noise shakes the color librarian from his reverie. It is uncommon but not un-familiar—the scrape of a manhole cover as it's dragged over the asphalt. The color librarian stands in the church doorway watching them crawl out. A boy. Then a girl.

Toiling away in the library basement, sorting the color into glass jars, he often imagines those hiding in the sewers as dirty, hunchbacked and blind, crawling out of manholes like radioactive megafauna, speaking in garbled grunts and moans. He can't help but feel a little disappointed they are fair and lithe with childlike faces, taking in the scenery like tourists. They look happy.

Only a few dozen are left, maybe a hundred, the color librarian estimates. The last of the believers, gone to search for a new Eden in the sewers, afraid of this humpty dumpty world. The color librarian likes to imagine that when they're not coming up here to scavenge they sit in the dark without joy or grief or surprise and sing hymns, recite prayers, play pinochle. He knows she is still there, carrying with her the memory of all this color.

And the others? The ones who laughed at those going into the ark? The ones who burnt the sky launching bombs hoping it would erase the rainbow? The ones who left in the military convoys? Is it true they escaped into interstellar space? Or did they die in a ditch along the highway, coughing up their insides as the stars blinked at them indifferently?

The boy and girl stand under a dusty lamppost. They're too busy admiring the rainbow to notice the color librarian. They take turns whispering about what they see in the color spectrum. She says a flower. He says a hand reaching down. They are quiet. Then the boy says one of the old gods put the rainbow here as a bridge between this world and the other, and on cold winter nights he meets his lover halfway across the arc and they share an ice cream cone. That's love, the boy says. He leans to kiss her but the girl bends away, folding her arms across her chest. What flavor of ice cream is it? she wants to know.

THE color librarian closes his eyes. When he opens them the rainbow is still there, but the boy and girl are gone.

The color librarian looks down the manhole into the black. He wonders if the boy and girl will be forgiven for their negligence. He drags the manhole grate over the hole. He walks to the end of the street, circles back. Uncovers the manhole. He sits cradling the bucket of color, legs dangling into the black. It must be easy to find your way in all that dark, he thinks.

The air is rancid, his throat burning from the colorless fumes. For reasons he cannot explain he respects the cruel honesty of this place. Later, he will go down to the basement and pour the dust into jars and try to sleep a few hours before waking up and starting all over tomorrow. But for now he waits, amazed how everything looks naked under this awful miracle of light.

Translation Folio

DIMITRA KOTOULA

Translator's Introduction

Maria Nazos

My years of translating the Greek poet, Dimitra Kotoula, have been pleasurable, complex, and seemingly insurmountable. The project began in an unlikely place: I was a first-year PhD student at the University of Nebraska-Lincoln, sitting in the office of former U.S. Poet Laureate, Ted Kooser. After taking Ted's fall semester poetry tutorial, despite our 40-year age difference and zero aesthetic overlap, we developed an improbable kinship which we uphold to this day.

It was Ted who suggested that for my upcoming independent study I translate a younger, Greek female poet.

Why? I asked. I was initially disappointed, as I'd wanted my work to remain center-stage.

Because he said, we can only have so many translations of Elytis, Seferis, Ritsos, and Cavafy. That seemed as good an explanation as any. From there, Ted—who ironically hasn't been out of the country—reached out across oceans to contact some friends who led us to Alicia Stallings, who lives full-time in Athens, who recommended Dimitra. From thereon, two more new relationships were formed.

I had no idea that I'd spend the next six years translating Dimitra, or what a delight, joy and challenge her poems would be to re-create. She and I are, as Alicia Stallings observed during the Sewanee Translation Workshop when we finally met in person, "Very different writers."

Dimitra's primary themes include the Greek financial crisis and the ars poetica. She writes as much about Greece's collapse as she does the poet's internal condition. The Poet, as depicted in "Cavafy Tries to Forget," struggles against his erotic memories and present desires. In this instance, the narrator pushes against memory to resist his current unquenchable thirst.

Throughout the "Case Study" poems, the Poet could arguably be Cavafy, too, as Dimitra has even said. To me, the Poet is a visionary, a witness, and unreliable narrator. In "Case Study VII," the Poet confesses, "I carry with me/ visible holes/ - the grit that follows me when I walk-" These lines allude to how poetry and the Poet evade the regular narrative, creating gaps and fissures wherever she goes. I'd also argue that in, "the grit that follows," the narrator alludes to the messy history and refracted memories which trail her, not unlike those which appear in "Cavafy Tries to Forget."

"Three Notes for One Melody," on the other hand, takes a poet-as-witness approach as she confesses, "Truth is that I like to watch . . ." The speaker then enacts another one of the author's thematic obsessions: going back in time to negotiate history. She describes confronting "the forefathers." Again, we see the narrator's desire to examine a once-thriving Greek empire, along with those historical poets. In so doing, the speaker feels, "a living sob/that tries to break away from me." Once again, history and memory present an ephemeral bridge the Poet attempts to cross. Isn't every writer's plight? Aren't we a chasing, re-imagining, and unearthing the genius of writers past? Aren't we forced to return to the present world and accept that we're trying to do the good work, each and every day?

As a bicultural woman who originally hails from my sea captain father's Mykonos and Athens, Greece, when I was thirteen my family and I relocated back to my Midwestern mother's Joliet, Illinois. I have never fit in either place. Only now, ironically in Lincoln, Nebraska, have I begun to feel at home. My translations and poetry have blended these geographical boundaries. These translations led me to break my 10-year hiatus when I returned to Athens, my former home, my main reason being to meet Dimitra in-person. There was however, another reason behind my six-year commitment to these translations, and for my return to Greece. When I slip back into that country and language, as the poet in "Three Notes for One Melody II" describes, there's my own history to confront. Going back to Athens meant reliving complex memories of my mother's unhappiness and mental break, and my parents' tumultuous relationship. That same need to unearth the past, just as Kotoula's narrator does, led me back to an Athenian coffee shop sitting across from the poet herself. We still try to meet once a year in between our frequent emails, to continue a friendship which extends beyond poems and oceans alike.

This semester-long independent study turned into a six-year book-length project. I've since taken my PhD, embarked upon the professional world, and never looked back. Still, I continue to work with Dimitra. This project, of course, hasn't always been easy. Dimitra has even said of her own work, "It is a puzzle, even for the most experienced translators." She and I in turn, have cultivated a friendship that's more than a friendship. Ironically, the difficult, intimate, satisfying bond we've forged can't be translated into language. She knows the sordid and joyful details of my life and I hers; yet we've only met in-person a few times. Perhaps this relationship is the one thing that can't be translated. Dimitra and I were working together as my six-year-relationship ended, as she endured the height of the Greek financial crisis, as the entire country's ATM machines refused to dispense more than 60 euros per person each day. It was Dimitra to whom I sent my wedding photos, and Dimitra whom I wrote to when I secured an exciting new job offer. I'll still be there, moreover, when her daughter, who was just a little girl when we began the project, will enter University. Now, as the poet encounters an aesthetic shift, my brushstrokes will re-imagine those poems, too. There aren't words for this relationship, aside from one: Translationship; I happen to think it's a good one, or at least the only one.

Case Study VI (On Poetry)

The sun spreads an intelligent shadow over the reliefs.
Sweaty summer sky descends.
History persists—
(just think: a piece of your life
has now finally come full circle)
like a bothersome gadfly.
The mystical one shines with his God
and the soul of things
-O, blessed gadfly-
knows the poem
and like a thin breeze
settles below its dome.

Case Study VII (the Poet)

I carry with me
visible holes
the grit that follows me when I walk
the chill on my shoes
things
that I did not say
I did not do
that if told
there I would be
face-to-face
concrete
no shadows.

•

It is well here
in the princedom of words.
It has a view of blankness
and I can
think or not think
at will.
The damage that I cause
heals easily
from the gift of cast aside words
which
-in extreme oscillation-
I return to you
for I no longer know what to do with them.

•

When I talk about verses
I speak of something that happens
to you as much as to me—
by entrusting my soul
to the fate of the Greek vowels

by offering myself over
to the next myth
I wrote
for a reason having little to do with language
even less from desire or passion
but because this was the humblest way
to live.

Cavafy Tries to Forget

*"From Time. All these things are very old—
the sketch, and the ship, and the afternoon."*
                                    C. P. Cavafy

*A momentary sensation of something unforgettable
a drunkenness from the present word entering the mind's rapture
and the "murmuring stream" (sic) of his lover's hands
already on his body.*

•

The sea is too far away
for him to fetch it here now
and the relaxed air of afternoon
just holds whatever he sees
what he so casually sees without images

Passion
—or maybe something not quite—
renews desire.
Remnants of silence settle in the room
(the empty air in that square room)
creating silence
and he wonders
if he is indeed here where he resides
"the high so worthless
the beauty
clear thought of other times."

Sometimes
—what could have been said
if there were words strong enough?—
he seems to be reminiscing again
of those long summer afternoons
when thought
having returned for a while
seems to withdraw

(the youth unclasps his hair
banishes memory
face dampened by laughter
with bite-marks yet from the light
beneath the flesh)

and he wonders
if he truly resides here
where he is
in this passionate piece of time
that is usually called body—
your body
while he resists incessant versions
of this poem
within it already—what;
this very thought of nothing
something
not strong enough
that still recants
the narrow row of trees outside his window
the deafeningly blue sky and the drawing
all that he tries to deny without reason
the source of his love

•

Look—
it smiles at him already
the ultimate masterpiece
and its slightest ripple
can free him
and its slightest ripple
can retrieve from inside him
within syllables of blood
that torment his temples

a little joy
scattered stars

Three Notes for One Melody

*"it is the greatest amongst herbs
and becometh a tree."*

H. D.

Truth is that I like to watch
slipping deeply back in time
into the forbidden chambers
with the ancient remains
of the forefathers.
I've not become any wiser
but I love to let myself get carried away
as the summer clarion fades
by the splendid chords of forgotten poets.
And I gracious or even wretched
long for the living sob
that tries to break away from me
crawling through the dark
shifting balances
seeking an infinite
more rich emotional sky.

Truth is
that I still insist to claim
gently
distant
as a lily if you wish
that ultimate
the only destination
which leads nowhere
to no spring
has no death
no time or sun
in the answer.

translated from the Greek by Maria Nazos

SARA MICHAS-MARTIN

Lalochezia

[noun] The use of vulgar or foul language to relieve stress or pain.

I leach a little helplessness
into the air today
emerging from the deep flu
now respiratory
in general stuck mode
behind on everything
I need to show up
brightly
with my erupting cough
for my young son
to get him to do things
like wash his hands
without saying: *can you wash*
your fucking hands.
The virus cleaves
to the nylon hairs
of my toothbrush
so I throw it away
make it vanish
inside the black garbage bin
the gateway to underworlds
of trucks and ferries
piled matter and rot
that for hundreds of years
will occupy the ocean's darkness

while particulates
stray back to us
through the soft bodies of fish
or through our home sinks
where we fill our cups
and rinse out our mouths.
The toothbrush in this story is red.

How to Become Invisible

It's not that people don't care about mothers
it's that they can't see them
after the bones have been relieved
of so much calcium   a new mother
is a doubled up idea   muddled in diameter
who presents socially as a team
but mostly is alone   plugged in
to the sockets of the house   body sourcing
its history of fevers   while the kitchen
swells with plates   she wants to sleep
a little in each room like a cat
without that weight   no cry-rupture
or damp bruising with the let down
before it's time again to latch   mammalian swirl
the lift   a wave breaking
her far centers cored and sucked out
frame hollowed   mere shadow
and that too   folds in
enters the straw

2 A.M. City

With the swaddle   be strict
the baby's hands
are matches flared by reflex
the baby's hands—
daggers that accident the face
hunger pries these hours
I fight the dropping off
all sleep is broken sleep
stalked by crying
or for too long   a non-crying

the door bell rings   and rings
purple cat   purple cat
what do you see?
I see a boy/man
looking at me
in here   alone
holding 10 pounds of crying
a lion is a cat   a cat a form of lion
be a gone cat
please   just be gone.

JENNIFER BROWN

Objects Not Arranged for Painting

Half-empty bottle of red wine, its
cork end-balanced on the table. Copper
tea-cosy distorts, reflecting convexly.

White shallow bowl, a couple of waxy plums,
dull & thumb-smudged. No glow from within,
no haze of rosy or blue or golden light,

no sculptural weight nor balance. Just this
arrested disarray & quiet clamor,
electrical hum & the shush of vents,

a visible docket of tasks, the plotted
points of dailiness. Just this egg-trove
of upturned kiwi-fruit—tart green &

brilliant in sackcloth skins, each one's umbilical
scar marking a lost way to its core.

PETER COOLEY

The Monkeys, the Monkeys; an Anniversary Poem

Our days come so they may go away.
We have so few, and who can stop to count?

This sounds like the beginning of a villanelle!
No, no, I want pentameter to stop!

There, I've stanched it.
On the morning dresser, the mourning

dresser, down the dawn-blue
first light, two little monkeys

I bought you at that eponymous coffee shop.
One gold-gray, in imitation

 of my graying, the other the color
(I see I fall into pentameter

by habit!) your hair kept, the auburn hue
that poet referenced in "The Nut-Brown Maid."

The monkeys intertwine.
Did I lay them out that way?

Did you, before I found you
in the identical blue-dawn light

a year ago, today, March 15th,
splayed on the couch,

your tongue hung across your lower lip?

I knew before I touched your cold forehead—
rhyme lets me say it. And pentameter.

I knew you were dead.

SARAH BARBER

To be a hill

be left behind, erode something,
or stare deep into the rock
until it faults. Rise up a little, somehow;
lump; then mound monotonous
and slow. You must resolve yourself
to stop sooner than an alp
where incautious spaniels released
from carriages to relieve themselves
are eaten by wolves.
You must resolve yourself
to being more easily walked.

—Or else consider, as a dome
is just a cup turned upside down,
you are the obverse of a hole
in which, if a man can see the sky,
he may plant potatoes.
            Yes,
you might have liked to be dug
in prettier ground—under a willow,
in turf set with violets—
but for some months before subsidence
the dead are so light under you
they almost float.

PAMELA ALEXANDER

Float

1
Half a walnut shell,
birthday candle mast—

light it, light it
before it drifts away

2
Rented rowboat, wooden
oars, oarlocks bronze—

my mother in the stern
tossing bread to mallards

3
Eighteen feet of fiberglass
sailing the Charles basin,

shallow water stapled
between Boston bridges

4
Wasa, thirty foot sloop,
Was a boyfriend who,

seasick at anchor, left
for good, for good

5
Kayak light enough
to portage solo, no deck,

open like a walnut shell—
paddler the upright

candle, mind
on fire with memory

Translation Folio

MESÁNDEL VIRTUSIO ARGUELLES

Translator's Introduction

Kristine Ong Muslim

THE THREE POEMS, WHICH I translated from the Filipino for this *Copper Nickel* feature, have appeared in their original language in *Ilahás*, the second book of Mesándel Virtusio Arguelles. The poetry collection *Ilahás*, a sequence of 43 poems, was published in 2004 by High Chair, a now-defunct Manila-based small press collective. After his second book in 2004, Arguelles went on his way to write 18 more books of poetry and essays, as well as one novel slated to be published soon. Arguelles teaches literature and creative writing at the De La Salle University, a private educational institution in Manila.

The term "ilahás" means "wild," but I decided to translate it to "feral" to capture a quality that gets dropped in translation when "wild" is used. "Feral" does not only encompass the full import of "wild" as it is used in Arguelles's book. It also connotes a return to primitive savagery after a period of being domesticated, and some of the poems in the book support this reading and my preferred translation.

The bulk of the poems in *Ilahás*, most strikingly in the poem "Doppelgänger," show Arguelles in peak form before his creative energies were diverted to erasures and other text-based experimentations that explore the various emotional and philosophical registers of modern isolation, as well as the formation and consequent erosion of identity. "Doppelgänger" is so intriguing and provocative in its attempt to examine rambling dichotomies that Filipino poet Marchiesal Bustamante wrote three poems in response to it some years later in the poetry collection *Mulligan* (2016).

The Filipino concept of "doppelgänger" is most prevalent in the belief that a doppelgänger is a harbinger of death—i.e., someone who sees his or her double is bound to die. Additionally, the lore of the indigenous Tagbanua tribe talks of a mythical creature called *balbal*, which steals corpses. The balbal steals the corpse during the wake and eludes detection by replacing it with a banana stalk. The banana stalk acts like a doppelgänger. People attending the wake won't see the banana stalk, but a dead body in the likeness of the corpse already spirited away by the balbal. The only way to know for sure that a corpse is what it should be—and not replaced by a banana stalk brought in by a balbal—is to pass it through an open window.

The poem "Cul-de-sac," consistent with the otherworldly and surrealist themes in *Ilahás*, is a meditation on the nature of art, the very human impulse that drives its creation, and its dreamlike intrusions into the material conditions of reality. Arguelles's other books, most notably *Hollow*, an upcoming bilingual volume from Fernwood Press, and *Walang Halong Biro* (De La Salle University Publishing House,

2018), another bilingual volume, have been revisiting in varying degrees these lines of inquiry.

In "Body Bag," the speaker is the body bag itself, and it mulls over not just the cadaver it is doomed to encase and embrace, but the weightiness of death's impact to the kin of the deceased: the persistence of grief as well as the pang of loss, the stage of denial, and then the ensuing numbness. The attention to detail in "Body Bag" is understandable and all too consistent with Filipino traditions around death and funerals, which vary across the archipelago. Among the most common Philippine superstitions surrounding death and funerals include taking a bath right after attending a wake so as not to track death throughout the home, as well as placing chicks on top of a casket to bring justice to a murdered person.

Doppelgänger

Nobody knows whether or not they had planned
their encounter

at the exhibit. Entirely irrelevant—
the art. Besides, it is unnatural

for doubles to meet.
They are not supposed to shake hands.

Because this confuses
the congruence between shadow

and shadow. Deters
scrutiny into the vulgarity

of ego and penile sizes.
To allay suspicion

of being watched and followed.
Thus the preemptive disclaimer

on denial—and conceit—
for self. Both being keen,

they slash each other's face;
they lament their resemblance; they disown

their likeness derived from god; and arrogate god
as form of creation. They should not have

clashed until
there's a limit. But then again,

it is also necessary to be in sync
with timing

and occasion: An encounter
for diverse stories wearing the same face.

Body Bag

I will bring home the corpse
of a stranger.
What sets apart a dead body
from another dead body?
Is it in the way one would absently touch
the enshrouding fabric, shocked,
grieving for kin,
for example?

Perception is deadened
by the temperament
of things.
Consider a dragonfly sharply turning
toward the shifting current
of prairie wind. Fluttering wings, insistent.

A combination of heft and buoyancy
makes hovering possible.
Against a round table, light crashes
as huddled minds fixate on drawing
cards. What line is being drawn?

Again, you open
the zipper. The snag catches
so you use tweezers.
Do not break off
for god's sake.
Beneath the shroud, a figure.

You close the zipper.
How does one slip
a splinter back into the thin
lining that separates skin
from flesh? Like before,
I get lost in the life
that gets taken from life.

Cul-de-sac

They culminated at the lowest point.
The depth of an empty cellophane bag.

They tried to turn around.
They found nothing:

but
the missing contents.

What else is left to be done
if returning is not possible.

They pore over the entirety of the
border. They try to pass through.

If all art
is unfinished.

The cellophane bag's integrity will be breached
by overburdening.

translated from the Filipino by Kristine Ong Muslim

ROBERT ARCHAMBEAU

Concerning the Soul of Andy Warhol

Warhol's work, though full of desire, is not full of feeling.
—Wayne Kostenbaum

People are often surprised to learn that Andy Warhol went to church every Sunday. Richard Townsend of the Dreihaus Museum swears Warhol's religion (Eastern Orthodox Catholic) ran deeper still, that the artist trekked off to mass almost every morning. It seems unlikely, given the rigors of Warhol's nightlife and social calendar, but it's not impossible: the house he grew up in was a pious one, with a brother who took vows and became a priest. And Jesus hovers over the artwork from the beginning to the end: a watercolor of the family living room Warhol painted when he was 19 or 20 features a crucifix, stark on the mantelpiece; and "Sixty Last Suppers," painted a few months before his death, makes a strong claim to be his last important painting.

Yet no one has ever thought of Andy Warhol as a soulful artist, or even as an artist with heart, whatever that may mean. Just as he was starting to make a name for himself in 1962, a panel of critics assembled at MoMa to talk this new Pop Art phenomenon into submission, and blasted Warhol as a prophet of spiritually desiccated consumerism. A half century later nothing had changed: "everyone," quipped cultural critic Jon Savage, "thinks he's emotionless and soulless." It was among Andy's intimates as it was among his enemies: Bob Colacello, who hung out and worked in Warhol's Factory for a dozen years, called him "the soulless soul of cool, the heartless heart of hip." When I told the poet Michael Anania I was about to write about Andy Warhol's soul, Michael asked "What's the idea—that he doesn't have one?" It took me a moment to formulate a reply. "Maybe so," I said, "but to treat that as something other than a problem."

•

"Nothing is more difficult than to realize that every man has a distinct soul," intoned Cardinal Newman, just as he was hovering on the verge of his great leap from high-church-Anglican to Catholic-with-a-convert's-zeal:

> . . . survey some populous town: crowds are pouring through the streets;
> some on foot, some in carriages; while the shops are full, and the houses

too . . . Every part of it is full of life. Hence we gain a general idea of splendor, magnificence, opulence, and energy. But what is the truth? Why, that every being in that great concourse is his own center and all things about him are but shades, but a 'vain shadow,' in which he 'walketh and disquieteth himself in vain.' He has his own hopes and fears, desires, judgments, and aims; he is everything to himself, and no one else is really anything.

The soul, here—as in much modern Christianity, Catholic or Protestant, is something uniquely individual, something like our core identity or special self. The notion comes, if memory of my one course on theology holds, from Greek philosophy's idea of the psyche, absorbed into Christianity at some point during its long tenure among the Romans and Byzantines. If this is what 'soul' is, did Andy Warhol have one? The answer stays 'no' for a long time before it comes out the other side as 'yes.'

Warhol was famous for his blank affect, what his pal David Bourdon called his "cool, eye-ball-through-the-wall, spaced look." His signature conversational gambit in opinionated Manhattan was to respond to any sort of assertion with a quiet, vague, wide-eyed "oh . . . yeah." He noticed it himself, this vacuum in the place where we generally find a personality: "I'm sure I'm going to look in the mirror," Warhol once said, "and see nothing." A case could be made that this was simply a matter of necessary guardedness. Warhol had, after all, been born gay, into a devout blue-collar family, in 1928: any core identity or special self he had was going to need some armor. I can see how the argument for a strong soul hidden beneath stronger armor would come together. All we have to do is look at Warhol's private drawings and sketchbooks of the 1950s, full of men's faces, nipples, feet, and genitals rendered with more dreamy, soft eroticism than you'd think a ballpoint line could muster. Even the style seems to come from a queer tradition: Warhol's 1955 sketch of James Dean could be one of Cocteau's drawings, were it not for the flipped-over sports car in the background. But the Tanager Gallery nixed a proposed Warhol show when the owners saw a drawing of two men kissing. So a year later, when the Bodley Gallery took a chance for a Warhol show called *Studies for a Boy Book,* the eroticism was oblique, veiled, muted (the book itself never appeared). Even the New York art world of the fifties didn't embrace queer identity the way it later would. Warhol noticed that Jasper Johns and Robert Rauschenberg didn't like him, and asked his mentor the underground filmmaker Emile de Antonio why. The reply was blunt: "You're too swish, and that upsets them," de Antonio said. Warhol was embarrassed to hear it. He claims he decided not to care, but opinions on whether he achieved that goal vary. Wayne Kostenbaum, looking back from 2001, found Warhol always a bit perturbed when admitting to homosexuality, hesitating "as if it were tacky." Significance could be drawn from the self-portraits painted over with translucent camouflage patterns Warhol made near the end of his life. A queer soul, hiding in a cruel world.

But the argument founders on a simple truth: what Warhol wanted wasn't armor, a carapace to shield a rich, inner, private world. What he always longed for was erasure, a way to be vacant all the way through. If he had a blank mask, it became a blank face, a blank interior, a blank space where the inmost soul would have been. Blankness was, after all, one of the qualities he most loved in others. He loved it in the affectless voice of Christa Päffgen, stage name Nico, whose vocal performances with Factory house band the Velvet Underground take listeners to a noirish place where faux-Weimar junkie world-weariness drapes itself over something cool and robotic. He loved it in Taxi, a southern debutante who became a habitué of the Factory and enchanted Warhol with what he called her "poignantly vacant, vulnerable quality." She was, he said, "a wonderful, beautiful blank. The mystique to end all mystiques." He loved it, too, in "vacant, vacuous Hollywood," which he rhapsodized over as "everything I ever wanted to mold my life into. Plastic. White on white." And he came to love a blank vacuity in himself. "The more you look at the same exact thing," he wrote in *POPism*, his memoir of the sixties, "the more the meaning goes away, and the better and emptier you feel."

Warhol couldn't be alone—except when he was sleeping and couldn't be near anyone at all. Waking, he needed people around him. And when he loved people who didn't present as mysterious blanks, they were people whose personalities were so big that they blew some kind of circuitry and blacked out the entire room around them. It's why he loved tragic drama queens like Edie Sedgewick and Judy Garland. "To me," he said, "Edie and Judy had something in common—a way of getting everyone totally involved in their problems. When you were around them, you forgot you had problems of your own." For two decades Andy went to parties populated by the biggest of personalities almost every night: being everywhere and seeing everyone was his way of not being anywhere, of not being anyone at all. He'd look into a mirror and see nothing—nothing but the cocaine traces left by someone else, someone busy making the most marvelous drama for him to watch.

Warhol always said that Pop came from the outside, and his working methods seem designed to cut any kind of introspection short before it begins. He'd blast the same record over and over to clear thoughts out of his head while he painted, and by the mid-seventies he reports having gone full Elvis, watching as many as four television sets at once. He wanted to be a machine, he once told an interviewer—and machine automatism drew him from painting to filmmaking. "The camera has a motor," he said, "and you just turn it on and walk away." You didn't have to be there. You didn't have to be anywhere at all.

He'd become the most successful commercial artist in New York through self-effacement, loving how art directors would tell him what to do and how to do it. He could disappear into house style or the imperatives of an ad campaign. Later, when he was richer and more famous than any commercial artist, he wrote "When I think about what sort of person I would most like to have on a retainer, I think it would be a boss. A boss who could tell me what to do, because that makes everything easy when you're working." It's not the rich inner world of the fiercely independent struggling genius he was after, not personal vision, not the expression of *soul*. Kirk Douglas' Van Gogh in *Lust for Life*? Not for him. But ask if he'd take the wide-eyed vacancy of Jane Fonda in *Barbarella* and he'd tell you: "oh . . . yeah."

The formal expression of soullessness was the renunciation of all traces of the artist's hand. Even though he was happy to follow orders and work to a client's specs, Warhol was more of a fine artist when he was a commercial artist than he ever was afterwards, if by 'fine artist' we mean someone with a recognizable drawn line or painterly facture. Spend half an hour with his illustrations for shoe advertisements and you'll recognize his early hand instantly for the rest of your life. But he was always drawn to mass-produced objects as subjects for his artwork, and in retrospect it seems inevitable that he would adopt the techniques and the anonymity of mass production himself. A 1962 graphite and watercolor piece depicts a Campbell's soup can hanging over the neck of a Coke bottle—subjects he would return to after he abandoned the careful still-life drawing and shading with which they're rendered. "I still wasn't sure if you could completely remove all the hand gesture from art," Warhol said, "and become noncommittal, anonymous." Marcel Duchamp had done it already, of course, with his cheeky *Bicycle Wheel* and *Bottle Rack* and *Fountain*, but Andy needed a nudge. He got it from Emile de Antonio in a moment that became one of his most famous anecdotes, told and retold. Here's the version he gives in *POPism*:

> I poured Scotch for us, and then I went over to where two paintings I'd done, each about six feet high and three feet wide, were propped, facing the wall. I turned them around and placed them side by side against the wall and then I backed away to take a look at them myself. One of them was a Coke bottle with Abstract Expressionist hash marks halfway up the side. The second one was just a stark, outlined Coke bottle in black and white. I didn't say a thing to De. I didn't have to—he knew what I wanted to know. 'Well, look, Andy,' he said after staring at them for a couple of minutes. 'One of these is a piece of shit, simply a little bit of everything. The other is remarkable—it's our society, it's who we are, and you ought to destroy the first one and show the other.

The unadorned Coke bottle, without any trace of Pollock-y, DeKooning-esque brush-strokes or drips—it's our society. It's who we are. But what it isn't is Andy Warhol, as manifested by a recognizable gesture with pen or brush. It aspires to the condition of mechanical reproduction. It's the reverse-Pinocchio, where Andy begins as a real boy and ends up as an automaton, reborn as an art factory machine.

Warhol soon begins making work by suppressing the hand of the artist: he traces from projected transparencies, co-opts existing public-domain photographs, and hires assistants to produce repeated images via silk screen printing. Other Pop artists—Jasper Johns, say—can revel in painterly surfaces, but Warhol represses them thoroughly. Walk through a Warhol retrospective and you'll feel the cool anonymity get cooler until you turn a corner into a hall where his collaborations with Jean-Michel Basquiat hang. Basquiat's demotic oil stick scrawl will feel like someone popped a window in a nosebleed-dry and morgue-cold room, and a hot breeze is pouring in.

In the absence of the distinctive, expressive artist's hand, what pleasures does Warhol's work offer? The most striking phenomenon is repetition: series after series of near-identical images (Elvises, Marilyns, endless runs of Jackie O). The effect of series or repetition, says aesthetic theorist Sianne Ngai, is to reduce stronger emotional responses, to flatten them out. What becomes important about an image presented in a series is the moment of variation, when one thing looks a bit different from all the others. Warhol created countless images of beautiful, famous women, but the effect of the work isn't beauty; he obsessively returned to images of death and disaster, but the effect isn't sublime. Instead—by virtue of repetition with minor variation—the effect is to render some of the images . . . interesting. When we call something "interesting," says Ngai, we mean that it gives us "an affectively low-key response to minor differences perceived against a background of sameness." We're not moved, as we may be by an image in isolation. We're too saturated with images for that. Instead, we start noticing the differences. Here's Warhol's *Ethel Scull 36 Times*, a silk screen showing images of the New York socialite taken in a photo booth—look at number 25: she's almost invisible in the dark blue. And doesn't she seem self-conscious in frame 30? And here, in *The American Man (Portrait of Watson Powell)*, where all 32 silk-screened images are the same, look at the slight errors of registration or background color. Doesn't the one near the middle on the bottom feel overexposed? Huh. Oh . . . yeah.

No one had done quite the same thing before—or, more accurately, no one had ever made deliberately inexpressive repetition into an instantly recognizable signature style. And it is here that the soul of Andy Warhol returns. If the soul refers to something original or special to us, intrinsic to our unique and irreducible identity, then the vacuity of affectlessness, embraced and exalted, is the essence of Warhol's soul. And it finds full expression in the repetitious, characterless surfaces of his art. Warhol, we might say, follows the *via negativa* of soulfulness. Just as he gained complete control over interviewers by saying he had nothing to say and demanding they give him answers to repeat back, his self-abnegation becomes the claiming of voice, agency, and distinctiveness. He finds his soul's special, blank character by renouncing any character at all. Is Warhol's a beautiful soul, or a sublime one? I don't know. But it is one quite unlike the fraught, turbulent souls belonging to the string of geniuses from Caravaggio to Rothko preceding him in the history of art. It is, in this context, a most interesting soul.

•

THERE ARE, OF course, other notions of the soul—old, durable ones that survive from millennia before Cardinal Newman's day. Consider the *népeš* (Hebrew: נֶפֶשׁ), a word most commonly translated in the King James Bible as "soul." Sometimes, though, the translation is "life," which gets closer to what was meant. The King James version of Genesis 2.7 settles on both: "And the Lord God formed man of the dust of the ground, and breathed into his nostrils the breath of life, and man became a living soul." It's an animating force, but not merely in that it brings life to the lifeless clay of flesh: it is life in that it is whatever someone desires or loves. It's what gets you out of bed in the morning. "It escapes at death," writes theologian Geddes MacGregor, "normally through the mouth or nostrils, although possibly on the point of a sword." To know Warhol's soul, then, is to know what he loved. One of the things he loved was fame.

Anyone who knew Andy knew this. Emile de Antonio said, somewhat apologetically, "it's an American disease to love famous people and Andy shared it." The critic Robert Hughes said Andy became "a conduit for an American state of mind whose idea of sacredness is celebrity." The *New Yorker*'s Calvin Tomkins wrote that Andy "pursued fame with the single-mindedness of a spawning salmon," a notion confirmed by Warhol's own report that "everyone always reminds me about the way I'd go around moaning 'oh, when will I be famous, when will it all happen?' so I must have done it a lot."

All fame was curiously equal: Chairman Mao, Liz Taylor, the electric chair, Howdy Doody: fame was a universal solvent that absorbed and neutralized any ideology, any endeavor, anything at all. But fame was more than that: for Warhol, a Slovak coal miner's son growing up sickly outside Pittsburgh, the world of the movies and glossy magazines was a kind of heavenly kingdom, a world somehow better and more real than the pinched and sooty streets around him. It's no accident that his 1962 *Gold Marilyn Monroe*, in which the brightly colored face taken from a publicity photo sits in a vast field of shimmering gold, is done in the manner of the devotional icons of the Eastern church. Indeed, Warhol's use of the same Marilyn photo for more than fifty other artworks—he never used another—has, in its repetition and fidelity, something of the devotional act about it. And the creed was decidedly that of fame: after his earliest period, Warhol rarely depicted anyone who wasn't rich or famous or a Factory "superstar," unless that person had achieved a momentary fame through death or disaster.

The amazing thing, for Warhol, was that one could become intimate with this other, shimmering world. This could happen when the façade of celebrity slipped, and we saw behind the curtain of glamor—Warhol once defined a good photograph as "one that's in focus and of a famous person doing something un-famous." We could also enter into a kind of communion with fame by virtue of participating in the same mass culture celebrities did: the sacramental wine being that most ubiquitous of American drinks, Coca-Cola. Just listen to Andy go on about it:

> What's great about this country is that America started the tradition where the richest consumers buy essentially the same things as the poorest. You can be watching TV and see Coca-Cola, and you know that the President drinks Coca-Cola, Liz Taylor drinks Coca-Cola, and just think, you can drink Coca-Cola, too. A Coke is a Coke and no amount of money can get you a better Coke than the one the bum on the corner is drinking. All the Cokes are the same and all the Cokes are good. Liz Taylor knows it, the President knows it, the bum knows it, and you know it.

He continues the sentiment in the passage from *The Philosophy of Andy Warhol* that comes closest to living up to the title's promise of delivering the Warholian ethos:

> Sometimes you fantasize that people who are really up-there and rich and living it up have something you don't have, that their things must be better than your things because they have more money than you. But they drink the same Cokes and eat the same hot dogs and wear the same ILGWU clothes and see the same TV shows and movies. . . . you can have the same nightmares.

The more intimate the connection with the world of fame, the better: Warhol once fantasized about a store where you could buy underwear worn by famous people— five dollars a pair if they'd been washed; fifty if they had not. This part of Warhol's soul burned bright until the very end: the assistant who took him to the hospital in his final days reports Andy asked, on admission, "Are there any famous people here?"

But fame wasn't the only thing Warhol loved, the only desire stirring in his soul. There was also family—not biological family (with the exception of his mother, he kept his distance from them) but the family of junkies, drag queens, street poets and misfits he convened around himself in the Factory in the years leading up to his shooting. The Factory scene burst into full flower in the summer of 1964. Instead of leaving town, as he had the year before, Andy stayed in New York. "Where could be more fun than this," he wondered, "with everybody you know coming by all the time, and you're getting work done? It was a constant open house, like the format of a children's TV program." A singularly louche children's program—Warhol sought out people who manifested as big performers of their sexuality, their traumas, their resentments and addictions. Drag queens were one kind of favorite, junkies another: some did duty as both. It was all a show for Warhol to watch. When the Factory folk were on drugs—and they were usually on drugs—Warhol reported as many as twenty dramas a day going on. One regular, he reports, "was always so high on speed that any little thing could send her into an hour-long monologue and I'd just sit there and watch the show."

Andy himself was never center stage: he was the audience, quiet, to the side. He was passive, or seemed to be. People in the world of BDSM have a term for what he did: topping from below. This occurs when someone, apparently submissive, finds ways to turn the seemingly-dominant others into the instruments of his or her fantasy, to control the scene from the sidelines, with no apparent agency. The Factory was like that; so was the traveling retinue Andy took with him to parties. The making of Warhol's movies juiced the dynamic to its maximum: often unscripted, the shoots were a matter of Andy assembling big personalities, provoking drama, and disappearing behind the camera while the bonfires of persona flamed. He was always in control, or felt like it, even when he should have seen the warnings—like when a big, rough young man who'd been a roadie for rock acts started coming by to "stomp around the Factory, grab me, and rough me up." It was outrageous, said Andy, and "I loved it, I thought it was really exciting."

The scene came to an end abruptly in June of '68, when Valerie Solanas strode into the Factory, took aim, and shot Warhol, nearly killing him and sending him to the hospital for months. The Factory family was disbanded before he got out. Some of the people he'd felt closest to were forbidden to visit: family or not, they were junkies, and he knew they'd steal his pills. Warhol worried the loss of the family would be the end of his life as an artist. "I was afraid that without the crazy, druggy people jabbering away and doing their insane things, I would lose my creativity," he confessed, "after all, they'd been my total inspiration since '64, and I didn't know if I could make it without them." He kept working, of course, and became ever richer and more famous—but the critical consensus is that the great period was over. Even his beloved assistant Gerard Malanga says that Warhol ceased to be a genius and devolved into something of a court painter for the rich.

Seven years after the shooting, Warhol seemed lost, nostalgic. "In the sixties everybody got interested in everybody," he wrote, but "the seventies are very empty." If the soul is the *nép̄eš*, the concentration of what we love, a part of Warhol's soul died in the summer of '68, departing not on the tip of a sword, but with a bullet.

•

THERE IS ANOTHER soul to consider, for which a name remains elusive—call it the Romantic soul, the cultivated soul, perhaps the humanistic soul. It's spiritual, sure, but definitely secular, and it has something to do with our sensitivity, especially our sensitivity to high art. It's not a kind of soul Andy Warhol cultivated. It may well be that it's something (and I write this as an observation, not a judgement) he helped to kill.

This type of soul died young, as notions of soul go, at least according to the Italian novelist Alessandro Baricco, who writes about it as a something people cultivated via a loving immersion in the traditions of the high arts:

> We call *Humanism* that extremely long moment during which, in inheriting intuitions that came from afar, an intellectual elite began to imagine that man had in himself a spiritual horizon traceable to something other than religious faith. . . . It was patented by the nineteenth-century bourgeoisie. They were the ones who made accepted fact the certainty that the human being had, in himself, the breath of spiritual reflection and preserved, in himself, a higher, noble, distant horizon. And where did he keep it? In his mind. . . . They needed this . . . they were not *destined* to power and greatness. They needed to find this destiny within themselves, to show that they indeed possessed a certain kind of greatness without needing anyone to grant it to them—neither men, nor kings, nor God.

They may not be nobles, they may not be Christians, but, goddammit, they knew they were special, because they knew they had soul. They knew it when something inside them stirred to the chords of Beethoven; they knew if more when they recognized in Brahms a stirring with its origins in Beethoven; they really knew it when they heard in Stravinsky a fist-shaking objection to the sounds of Daddy Beethoven and Papa Brahms—sensitivity echoing with sensitivity through the long corridors of their cultivation. This type of soul is not something Achilles would have understood—or Dante, for whom soul was an emanation of the divine.

To understand the relation of the humanistic soul to cultivated taste, says Baricco, we need only think of William Faulkner:

> To enter into one of Faulkner's books, what do you need? You need to have read many other books. In a certain sense, you need a mastery of all of literary history: a mastery of literary language, a familiarity with the temporal anomaly of reading, an acceptance of a certain taste and a certain idea of beauty that have formed over time within the literary tradition. Is there anything external to book culture that you need in order to make the journey? Almost nothing. If nothing at all existed except books, Faulkner's books would remain essentially quite comprehensible.

Pop Art, much like pop culture as a whole, works otherwise. It's easy to see if you glance at a list of best-selling books. Do this, Baricco maintains, and "you'll find an incredible number of books that wouldn't exist if they didn't start from a point outside the world of books." You'll find mysteries and thrillers that can be enjoyed without a deep knowledge of literature: indeed, the instructions on how to appreciate them are generally absorbed through watching television. You'll find celebrity tell-alls, for which the meaningful context isn't a line of literary descent running from *Beowulf* to Virginia Woolf, but the gossip magazines. You'll find books that are offshoots of movie or video game franchises. Instead of following a horizontal axis that bores deep into literary history like a rock drill, such books send you along a horizontal axis, skimming away from literature *per se*, skipping like a stone thrown the across the smooth surface of the contemporary.

The instructions for appreciating Warhol's *Turquoise Marilyn* or *Mickey Mouse* aren't given in the history of art from the Renaissance to Rothko. We've already breathed in the instructions from the media atmosphere in which we move. "The sixties were about blurring boundaries," says the great art critic and Warhol fan Peter Schjeldahl, and Warhol blurred the boundaries between art and not-art, with works "keyed to supermarkets and movie magazines." Was what he made high art? From the perspective of someone unconcerned with the humanistic soul, the question isn't interesting enough to answer, may not even be comprehensible. Warhol, says Schjeldahl, made "glamour-industrial goods," and if you know how to love celebrity like Andy did, you know how to love them, too. The soul hardly enters into it. Breathe out in the chilly air and watch it go.

SARA BURNETT

Ab Ovo

so not from nothing, my yolk
        and hatchling, pomegranate jewel
                set in membrane, clot and thread,

honey of the hive. I didn't know you,
        one of seven million chances
                hibernating in a fluid sac

waiting for the signal to implant
        yourself. Out of the vestibular bulb,
                the tulip, the peacock feather,

the fern. In another life, you were a crocus
        pushing up through snow. I was a doe
                crossing a busy stretch of road

alone. Unfurl your leaves, your top-heavy
        camellia head. You made a bed
                from pressed petals

in the swaddling dark. Your body was
        that supple. I kept a wad of soaked
                cabbage leaves to cool the sores.

Forgive the ways I'm ill-prepared
        to receive you, for you to break
                from this womanly body

into your own. In another life, I was the wind
        prickling your ear to keep you still.
                You were a deer in tall grass.

CLAIRE WAHMANHOLM

At the End We Turn into Trees

After we lost the child, it became too painful to have a face. Mine had eyes that kept
showing me *not her, not her*. There she wasn't in the garden, there she wasn't in the crib,
the park. Why hadn't those places disappeared along with everything she had ever
touched. I wanted every map to be lace, wanted atlases to crumble between their covers, for the cut-out pieces to be collected in vials and stored somewhere safe forever.
I wanted our house to be a scorched cathedral I wandered through. I wanted it to be
mostly air. Your face had her eyes, which was worse. You covered the mirrors and I
covered you. We lived like ghosts. Everything was a wound that needed to be burned
closed but I wanted to bleed out. I hoped for a curse, for some magic to interfere.
Then one night as we lay like rocks in our bed, the clock ticked past midnight and kept
going. A hole opened in the space between my exhale and inhale, and deepened. I
buried myself in my non-breath and let it close around me. Within those lung-woods,
a shadow against a darker shadow, a sense of movement, an edge. A witch, mother as
moss, who understood what I had come for. Not death, but a rest no mammal could
arrive at with its nerves and blood, its offspring living then not. I felt the witch's hands
on my calloused face, my coarsening shoulders, my heartwood spine. Then I didn't. I
hadn't for hundreds of years. Beneath our heavy featherbed of soil, we are reaching
toward each other. We are tangling without touching. Slow as sap, across the mycelial
threads I am sending you the smell of her hair, her teddy bear, her sheets. You are
sending her voice, crackling like lightning at one hundredth the speed. We soak in the
patter of her hopping feet, which is painless as rain. We make a wet, inhuman sugar
from the syllables of her name.

If Anyone Asks

By now I have so many and so much/ that fortune can't do harm
                                                        Niobe

                Do not compete with gods, and do not boast
                                        Ovid, *The Metamorphoses*

            I do not wake up buzzing with happiness.
In fact my bed is full of wasps. I have been stung

                everywhere tender. I have not had fun
                        in a long time, maybe in ever.

                My blessings do not run over and also
                    I have none. My sink is leaking.

                My sink is running over with wasps.
                They have carried off all my sugar.

See how poor I am, how luckless, how unshapely
    my head from which no hair falls in waves.

                        I have no children to speak of,
                no robes sewn with threads of gold,

            no robes. I am a patch of dirt, a glass
of vinegar, a bony goose among fat others.

    I am an unworthy enemy, small and mean.
    In fact calamity has already been and gone,

its arrows still clean. I do not need to play dead.
Not even death would want to play with me.

MICHAEL MARK

My Money Meets My Mother Two Years After She's Dead

She kisses and kisses them, the 1s as much as the 10s
same as the 50s as the hundreds. Every corner, star, leaf,
every wrinkle every serial number's number. She kisses
my checks my credit cards my three bank statements,
my You Just Won a Million Dollars junk mail, she kisses.
My mother is jubilant giggling so pale. She says what she
always sings when I visited, you are my sunshine my only
sunshine. She rubs Lincoln's beards onto her chin's white
spikes. I'm well, I'm well, she says and how's by you Abraham?
Lincoln kisses her cheek and she puts his mouth to her closed eyes
and—I can't hear what she says. She breaks into a puddle
of green flashes, semi-transparent, parts water, part sky, a standing
puddle of mother pride. And when she tires of her moaning,
what she would call kvelling, breathless, mere ripples, her voice,
vapor weak, almost dead, the pennies, she calls, where are my shiny
babies?

J. KATES

Betrayals

The trails I cut and cleared for thirty years
with labor and with love are overgrown
by hemlock, scrub, and mountain laurel. Deer
and coyotes make the paths their own.

The children, citified and settled up,
no longer care to try to find the fort
they built among erratics. From the top,
in olden days they held a mossy court

and ruled a realm as wide as everywhere,
buttressed with mud and sticks that still stick out
at unkempt angles from the ruins. (There
a melancholic could find food for thought.)

One mottled beech that marked a crossing lies
like fallen Saul across the way it once
defined. But even now, there's no surprise
for me—I walk those woods in confidence

that borders close on boredom, know too well
who left that stack of cordwood rotting on
a useless and abandoned crumbling wall.
No mystery—I meant to bring it in,

but let it go, season by season, till
it wasn't worth the work. Even today,
I started walking out with a good will
but turned aside and back, coming away

to write these words out of my head, *The trails*
I cut and cleared for thirty years . . . before
I'd lose those, too, among the small betrayals
of land, of stewardship, of memory.

KATHLEEN McGOOKEY

On I-96

When a dump truck passes us, we are not prepared for a horse's stiff leg sticking out, rising and falling like a lever pressed by an invisible hand. As she reads the truck's logo—Noah's Pet Crematory—my daughter stumbles on the last word. The large truck has high sides and a deep bed. Even when we look away, we can't forget the whole horse: it must be resting on many smaller, piled-up bodies. The white leg shifts in and out of view. The truck is white. Even the air around the leg is white. Above us, the clouds are so quiet.

Box

My parents' ashes are still in a cardboard box on the metal shelves in my basement. It's not all their ashes, just my share. They left instructions, but no deadline: when the dogwood blooms, on that trail near the pines. Sometimes I feel a slight pang—is keeping them like this undignified? Disrespectful? But then I forget them until I need the crockpot, and there it is, the little box, heavy for its size, labeled in my writing, next to my daughter's baby clothes. I haven't held it since we moved ten years ago. But I might. I could.

MAXIM LOSKUTOFF

Undersong

SHE STABBED ME BEFORE THE train even left the station. We were alone in the rear car, save for a fat man dozing in a dark green trench coat and a large crate which seemed to contain some sort of a cat. The Adirondack Express, overnight to Montreal.

I had been watching the fat man and the crate because they seemed in no way connected. The crate in the empty space at the front of the car, the fat man halfway back, and us pressed together in the final row of seats. She withdrew the blade as quickly as she had thrust it in—a single swift motion. I gasped, trying not to cry out.

The wound in my chest was clean. No pain, just heat and the feeling of air leaking in. The train jolted forward. The flanged iron wheels rolled along the track through the tunnels of Penn Station, and I was filled with the sense of the world seeping in. She dropped the knife.

The car shook. My vision swam. Rows of empty seats in front of us, two threads of fluorescent light along the ceiling, dark columns in the cement caverns flickering past the window. The fat man did not turn around.

"It wasn't necessary," I said.

The weight of the city heaved above us. The knife had fallen on the seat between our thighs.

"I don't even think you know when you're being cruel anymore."

The corner of her eye trembled. She picked up the knife and hid it in the folds of her skirt. Then she lay her long, bony hands flat on her knees. "I'll get out," she said. "In Yonkers."

The train burst from the underground into the lesser dark of Harlem. The black sky was punctured by soda billboards and a lone glowing cross. I reached across and took hold of her wrist.

She closed her eyes.

THE attendant leaned his face so close to mine that I could see his nostrils quiver with each breath. "Coffee? Tea? Danish?" The sparse whiskers above his lip trembled and he gestured with a gloved hand to the cart in the aisle behind him. Steam rose from two steel kettles. A basket was piled with pastries and dark red apples. "You're look-ing, sir, if you don't mind my saying, quite peaked."

I raised my arm to cover the wound in my chest. "It's this cold," I said. "Will it ever end?"

A blue pillbox cap was perched high atop the attendant's head. He smiled. His gray eyes moved across my hand on her wrist. Her body tensed. "You're simply traveling in the wrong direction," he said. "This morning I was in Miami." The antiquated cap—like something from a film—bobbed up and down when he spoke.

"Your family?" I asked. I wanted to keep him there. It was safer.

He shook his head. "In Poland. My father works the Silesia. Overnight from Krakow to Prague. If you think this is bad, the criminals there release gas into the cars. A powerful sedative. They rob the passengers while they're asleep."

He paused. His face was young but it was hard to say how young. Perhaps he was one of those who is never able to grow a proper beard.

"Something for you, ma'am?"

Her eyes gleamed in the shadows. Her lips parted. "You escaped?" she asked.

"I left," he answered. "My father is immune. He walks through the gas like London fog, dispensing blankets."

The whistle blew a long sad note as a deserted station flashed past, too quickly for me to catch the name. Hack or stack—one of the rickety Hudson towns. She ordered coffee. The attendant filled a Styrofoam cup, stirred it twice with a silver spoon, and handed it across my lap. She took the cup with both hands and lifted it to her lips. She inhaled the wisps of steam.

"What have we got in there?" I asked, nodding toward the crate at the front of the car. The attendant placed the kettle back on the heating coil. He smiled.

"An amazing creature. It travels to Central Park once a month to visit family at the zoo."

AFTER the attendant had gone, she punched me in the jaw. My head snapped back against the seat. Burning coffee sloshed onto my lap. She tried to wipe it away with trembling fingers.

I looked down at the spreading brown stain, something continental in its outline.

"You're a liar," she said, wiping her eyes. "All I asked was for you to tell me the truth."

The animal in the crate began to turn and growl. Its tail swished. Still, the fat man did not awaken. I had the feeling that when he did, it would be too late. Some men are born this way.

We were suddenly in a forest. The yellow moon shone between tangled branches. The trunks stood in neat rows, like an army preparing to advance. I opened my mouth and lied again.

She turned to the window, clasping the steaming cup. Her eyes followed the moon.

Rhinebeck, Cold Springs, Poughkeepsie. I leaned over and gnawed on her shoulder. My teeth ripped the fine silk threads of her shawl.

Using the bell suspended on the cord above our heads, she summoned the attendant.

"The railroad has rules for your safety, ma'am," he said. "Can you imagine if we let anything loose on the trains?" He shook his head. "The insurance alone."

"I just can't stand to see an animal locked up," she said.

"I can assure you," he said. "It's for the best."

The tracks curved around a bend in the river and the attendant steadied himself against our seat. The index finger of his white glove was stained with coffee. It cast doubt on the entire operation. He shook his head, the blue pillbox cap like the admonishing crest of a blue jay.

Was he eighteen? Twenty-five? Forty? Time changes when you're on the move. One day you step off a train and discover that all your friends have passed away.

"The company is well insured?" I asked.

The attendant narrowed his eyes in suspicion. "Of course. In accordance with both domestic and international law." The ringing of a distant bell summoned him. He left our car, glancing back at me before he disappeared.

"I'm going to let it out," she said.

"No, you're not," I answered, but the knife was in her hand again. She plunged it into my thigh. Surgical. Precise. She knew exactly how to incapacitate me. I clutched the wound with both hands. More air leaked in. I was like a ship taking on water. The horizon wobbled, maps slid across the deck. Fort Ann, Whitehall, Crown Point. We were hurtling into the darkness. I hunched forward. She climbed over me, her skirt and shawl askew.

"You're crazy," I said. "You bitch." I tried to follow her but my leg was useless. I smelled spilled coffee and her perfume. Dark mountains loomed in the distance. The trees crowded together.

She waved the knife over her shoulder as she walked down the aisle. Long black hair streamed behind her. She was as wild as the day I found her, beneath a statue in the park.

The fat man's head slumped on his chest. She passed him without slowing. She knelt in front of the crate. She looked back at me—her eyes wide, for a moment unsure—and then she unlatched the crate's gate.

The leopard poured out like water. It brushed past her and leapt to the top of the seat in a single bound: seamless and graceful, as if it had been planning its escape since before we left the station. A shadow, oil sliding over the lip of a cliff. It leapt into the luggage rack. Its paws padded above my head. It retreated to the farthest, darkest corner, where its yellow eyes glinted in the shadows.

My love stood in the aisle by the open crate, her mouth agape, her hair loose around her shoulders, shocked by what she'd done. The train's iron wheels rattled and hissed below us—that relentless, locomotive undersong. Crossing townships, counties, American mulch.

The trees broke apart in a sudden wash of cattails. Their tufted faces waved in unison in the moonlight. A lamp shone on the porch of a farmhouse.

"Come back," I said. "What have you done?"

I imagined her leaping out the window of the train. Scrambling through the marsh, knocking on the door. Finding someone home.

THE attendant refused to return to our car no matter how many times I rang the bell. "You let it out," he called through the door. "You put it back."

"It's unprofessional," I said. "We're ticketed passengers."

My love laughed from the seat in front of me. Her teeth were like pieces of chalk in the fluorescent light. The stained blue seat back was a buffer between our bodies. "You know, darling," she said. "It's more afraid of you than you are of it."

"Why do you want to hurt me?" I asked. I grabbed a lock of her hair. I wound it around my fingers. "This was supposed to be a holiday. We were going to have breakfast on the Rue Marquette."

Furious, she tore herself free. "Breakfast?" she hissed. The shawl slid from her shoulders and the knife fell to the floor as she scrambled over the back of the seat. She landed in my lap and sank her teeth into my cheek. I howled. The leopard cowered above us. The attendant watched through the single glass pane of the door, his ageless face transfixed.

"You're a fool, you're so afraid of being made a fool," she said.

"You're cold," I said. "When I look at you that's all I see."

She spat into my eye. I spat into hers. Saliva dribbled down our chins. I beat my fists against her rocky chest.

Finally, the leopard had enough. It leapt from the luggage rack and landed squarely on all four of its paws in the aisle beside us. The black fur along its spine bristled. Its yellow eyes flicked back and forth. A growl began deep in its throat.

The attendant pressed his face to the glass. "Now you've done it!" he called.

It was all a game to him, I could see that now. Coffee and Miami and a father striding through the gas.

My love and I pressed ourselves back against the window. I wrapped my arms around her; she intertwined her fingers in mine. Gray dawn light illuminated the ridge of the leopard's hackles. It stepped toward us. One huge, black paw.

"Please," I said. "We only wanted you to be free."

"If you're going to kill us, do it fast," she said.

The yellow eyes narrowed. The corners of the leopard's lips rose, revealing two long, gleaming incisors.

"Oh, my love," I whispered. I tightened my hand around hers. She breathed in quick, shallow bursts.

Suddenly, the fat man stood and lurched into the aisle, still bleary from sleep. The bulk of his shoulders filled the entire center of the train. His eyes were clouded by indulgent dreams, his cheeks blotched and rosy. He bunched his thick lips and whistled, turning himself red.

"Olga!" he called.

The leopard Olga stopped. She turned her head toward him. Her lips slid back over her teeth. Her hackles fell, she pivoted and padded toward him over the carpet.

He knelt and stroked her head. Ruffling the short fur behind her ears, smoothing down her hackles. "It's okay, my love. We're almost home."

AND he was right, for the three towers of Montreal appeared to the north: crystal spires against the reddening horizon. I could make out the outer embankments of the fortress and the castle's balustrade. Morning light stretched toward us. An arrow of geese flew across the sky.

The train rattled, beginning its slow, final refrain. Hoarfrost sparkled on the yellow sign at a crossing. Olga padded back into her crate. The fat man shut and locked the gate. We heard her rustling as she settled herself. Then the fat man turned toward us. He grinned. His figure seemed to grow even wider as the day came on. His shadow threatened to overtake the entire car.

"I can still remember," he said. "What it was first like to be in love."

Translation Folio

GUY GOFFETTE

Translator's Introduction

Marilyn Hacker

GUY GOFFETTE IS ONE OF the most unabashedly lyrical contemporary French poets. His work is suffused with humor, longing, tenderness, nostalgia and occasional cruelty; and he does not hesitate to hint, at least, at narrative. He makes use of the quirks of language to mirror the quirks of thought; his deployment of myth is never far from concrete and earthy evocations of childhood, of emotional loss or physical passion.

Guy Goffette was born in Jamoigne, in the Lorraine region, but on the Belgian side of the border, in 1947. This bit of geography has been sometimes French, somtimes Belgian, and the shifting and permeability of borders has always been among the poet's subjects. He lived in northern France for many years, and worked as a bookseller and as a schoolteacher. His austere and prematurely ruptured childhood is eloquently invoked in a book of literary memoir, *Partance et autres lieux*, published in 2000, which also sets forth some keys to his work:

> Once, I dreamed of leaving for the sake of leaving and I always returned.
> Now I leave without budging, and there is no coming back. You never leave,
> wrote Rimbaud, which could also be understood as: one never stops leaving,
> and the real journeys aren't the ones you'd think. That nonexistent sea be-
> yond the poplars is more real to me than the sea, and farther away than all the
> Abyssinias. It's enough to let myself go.

(Rimbaud's "On ne part pas" occurs more than once as a reference or an epigraph in Guy Goffette's writings.)

Nonetheless, he has traveled, both near—in France, Belgium and the Netherlands—and far, to Greece, to Eastern Europe, to pre-Katrina Louisiana. Like his friend and early mentor, the poet Jacques Réda, he is a jazz enthusiast. He lives now in central Paris, where he works as an editor at Gallimard. His poems often dialogue with others in the landscape of modern and contemporary French poetry—Jean Follain, Jacques Roubaud; as well as foreign poets, from Leopardi to Auden, Borges to Dickinson.

"A Little Gold in the Mud" is from Goffette's 1991 collection, *La Vie promise*, republished in 2000 in the Poésie Gallimard series. It was in that book where he introduced his signature 13-line sonnet variation, deployed in this sequence: three quatrains, most often (but not invariably) unrhymed, and a last line which sometimes, though not always, mounts to the classic 12 syllables of the alexandrine. The sequence is, also characteristically, at once imbued with longing—for an Elsewhere, any Elsewhere—, a vivid and tragi-comic sense of passing time, and what seems almost to be a celebration of acedia, a realization, (or is it a desire for it to be so?) that the Elsewheres of the imagination may be richer, or at any rate more accessible, than those we might, if not confined, travel to by train or plane and explore.

GUY GOFFETTE : A Sequence

A Little Gold in the Mud

And I said to myself too: to live is something more
than forgetting how time passes, and the ravages
of love, of wear and tear—what we do
from morning till night, cleave through the sea,

cleave through the sky, the earth, in turn a bird,
fish, mole, at last: playing at stirring up air,
water, fruits, dust; acting as if,
burning for; moving towards, harvesting

what? the worm in the apple, the wind in the wheatfield
since everything always falls back, because everything
begins again, and nothing is ever the same
as what was, neither better nor worse,

and keeps repeating: to live is something more.

In the time it takes to actually get up, to say
yes from your toes to the crown
of your skull, yes to this new day thrown
in time's wastebasket, it's raining.

O the soul's precise snapshot, those two words
that pierce our eyes like fingernails
in flesh: it's raining. The grass's blood
is unbearably green, and it's inside us

that it rains, inside us that a broken dike
sees slowly collapsing, behind the pane
between the curtains, with patches of old
regrets, hours exhausted waiting,

the reasons to leave and clothe the cold.

And still, if the fire were sputtering, if bitter
honey trickled from the lamp, you could say: I'm cold
and steal the bald walnut tree's heart, or
the heart of the workhorse with nowhere to go

and who goes from one end of the rain to the other
like you in the house, opening a book,
a door, pushing them away: scorched earth, open
city where famine spreads and cries out

like those clusters of red fruit on the table,
a foreign life, an inaccessible instant,
for the one who henceforth only knows
how to stamp his feet in that same furrow

the black and heavy clay of his fatigue.

Perhaps you ought to draw the curtains, let
your whole body sink into lassitude,
unknot thoughts' interlacings, the algae's
dark embrace, cut to the quick

of your own death, that which had been and
is no more, with what will come, the ineluctable
tide of sounds and images the drowning—they say
—don't take with them, let time

like the rain beat on your forehead
until everything becomes dust again
in the dead man's room: they empty the drawers,
sweep the floor, and through the open door, light

is momentarily made flesh and trembles.

They say: sunshine after the rain, the sea
after the mountain, love after
and to leave, to leave. Tomorrow when everything will be,
when everything will have, when.

Promises of the dead if living is more
than waiting, hoping. Ashes thrown
on the fire that grumbles a little then is still
and unconsoled: night

falls, dawn breaks, a summer has passed.
Already, says the hamlet's chimney-smoke
while animals, free of anger, continue
piling up the gold of time, the gold

of our eyes, avid and so swiftly closed.

And you end up putting the book on the shelf, up there
in its place, that little hollow of shadow and oblivion
like the plot of earth that comes back to you.
You come back, you too,

to your spot, in front of the window, the table,
that square of snow no one has yet defiled
and that goes every which way like your life
among words, among the dead.

You know very well that no sign will cure absence
any more than the blackbird, falling, reverses
earth's axis, but you persist, O scribe
in trying to bribe the angels:

a little gold in the mud, say, so the night stays open.

If I've been seeking—and what else have I done?—
it was the way one descends a steep-sloping street
or because all at once the birds
were no longer singing. That hole in the air

between the trees, neither my breath nor my eyes
filled it up—and I cried out often
standing amidst the weeds, but I wasn't waiting
for anything, I'd say to myself: there,

I'm in the world, the sky is blue, the clouds,
clouds, and what does the apples' muted cry
on the hard earth matter: the beauty of it is
that it will all disappear, and that, knowing it

everything nonetheless keeps idly strolling.

Toward the west, with the last rose-colored rays,
and following the arrow on the tight-stretched stocking
of night who's bent down to pluck and place
the airplane in her pocket, there's

what still holds you, eyes on the sky, standing
in this parking lot where in the gray light you fray
your Columbus' sails, your silk and
salt and solo roads, waiting.

Waiting for it all to be over (you say *all*
like someone whistling to keep his shadow close
on the darkened side street) all: this just-brushed
kiss of sunset on the lips

of the one on her way, who leaves the train platform to you.

What I wanted, I don't know. A train
passes in the night: I am neither on it
or outside. Everything happens as if
I lived in a shadow

that the night rolled up like a sheet
and tossed down the embankment. In the morning
extricate the body, one arm, then the other
with time throbbing

at the wrist. A train carries away
what I wanted: each window illuminates
another passenger in me
than the one I push away on waking

the wooden face, the crossties, death.

I'd say to myself: you still must, you must—
and the words would run ahead of me, sniffing
the road, the sky, the ferns, the nearly-
unbuttoned belly of the hills

and they'd come back, bringing me a scrap of
charred skin, a bone fragment, that old
and always obsessive question
why here? Why me ? Why?

—to go to come to wait like the station-master
of departures, who opens and closes the horizon,
waits for the last traveler to have gone
before turning the slate over, and writing:

closed because of laziness.

translated from the French by Marilyn Hacker

CAROLYN OLIVER

Consolation

MID-MAY AND THE RHODODENDRONS had already gone blowzy. Ada caught flashes of drooping pink as she smacked at the horsehair plaster next to the chimney. Three weekends left before school let out for summer (deliverance), three weekends she'd pour every hour stolen from grading into renovation. Then back to the island, to the Whaler's House, where she'd elbow her way into another life, become a widow for tourists' entertainment. Why don't you just relax, enjoy the summer off, her surgeon brother asked, practically dribbling envy. Money, she said, and that shut him up. Of all her colleagues, only the married teachers didn't have summer jobs, plus the ones who came from wealthy families, and she'd met precious few of those in twenty years. Without summers spent in itchy black dresses with mock whalebone corsets—as if someone might inspect her undergarments for authenticity—there'd be no money to renovate her house. And even when she finished this last room, something would probably break (ominous, the boiler's griping), and she'd be back on the wasp-ridden widow's walk for another blistering summer.

She misjudged the shovel's angle and sideswiped the chimney. A brick clattered to the floor in a haze of debris. Mercifully the lath beneath the plaster was undamaged—she hoped to avoid replacing it. She hunted for the brick, wondering why she'd never thought to check her chimney for artifacts, especially considering the one her student had found.

This was last year, three rooms ago, the week she was testing paint samples in the guest room, trying to find just the right shade of blue-gray, the color of the ocean under beach-emptying clouds. Her tenth graders were working on marsh ecology projects, but the whispers emanating from Preston Smart's huddled group suggested they were not making lists of invertebrates.

"I found it in the chimney," Preston blurted out when she reached for the box they scrambled to hide.

Ada expected a frog, or firecrackers, or some inedible lunch item meant for her desk. Wrong. Her brain, usually so reliable, needed a moment to register what she was seeing, so she asked, "What were you doing inside a chimney?"

"Nothing."

Her sharp gaze caught the scrapes high on his cheeks, near his ears, the bruises on his knuckles. "Nothing" probably meant being stuffed into the chimney by his brutish older brother. She suppressed a shudder, recalling Bailey Smart laughing, throwing loops of frog intestine down the front of Claudia Ward's dress.

"I'm going to confiscate this. Come see me after class if you want it back. Finish your lists."

She spent the rest of the period attempting to focus on post-field trip lesson plans. When the bell clanged, Preston scuttled out without meeting her eye. She locked the door.

Inside the box was the most exquisite example of scrimshaw she'd ever seen. Miniscule beach roses, mussel shells, gull feathers—all etched into the surface of a whale's tooth carved into a dildo.

Dildo. She toyed with the etymology for a moment, let it go. What a charmless word, especially for an object so lovely. In all her years on the widow's walk she'd never fathomed such a thing existed. The sailor who carved and inked it with soot on the long ship-bound nights must have been thinking of shore, of home. Or perhaps she shouldn't be so parochial; maybe his lover had made it.

She tucked it away in her desk, expecting Preston would summon the courage to ask for it back at some point, or write a note. But he never did, and amidst all the drama of Mr. Tannenhouse's removal, she decided it would be best to bring it home.

Ever since, it had lived in the guest room closet, protected in the cool dark. She ought to take it to a museum; it should be conserved. But what if the museum never displayed it? Some of the curators she'd met were so . . . unimaginative. At least she appreciated it, the whaler's beautiful, intimate object, meant to comfort, meant to last; the pleasure she'd found in the discovery of this solid piece of consolation and its delicate allure was matched only by her labor of love, this house with the wilting rhododendrons, a house someone else would someday break to pieces and remake.

And then she was wrapping the scrimshaw in soft cotton, waxed paper, sealing it tight. The replaced brick stuck out just a bit. Tempting.

KATHY FISH

Bear Walks into a Bar

BEAR WALKS INTO A BAR. Lisa and Carmen and Carmen's mother (who invited herself) have a table by the ladies room. The Moonglow used to be a supper club. Lisa's grandparents and Carmen's grandparents used to drink martinis here. It's just a bar now, with a dance floor.

Carmen asks to borrow Lisa's lipgloss. She's into the DJ but the DJ's not into her. Carmen's the heavy one. Her mother tells her she needs to reduce. I wish you were slim like Lisa, she says. Lisa would be lying if she said this didn't please her.

Bear walks into a bar to a burst of fireworks as if he's won something.

Lisa says to Carmen, I need you, baby. She hooks her finger in the belt loop of Carmen's jeans. A soft roll of fat bubbles over the top. Carmen is taller, broader, thicker than Lisa who doesn't need to reduce.

Bear cannot remember what drew him to this place. He was only hungry. Bears are attracted to scent. Maybe he smelled the trash that is Carmen's mother.

Lisa says to Carmen, come closer. They have been friends since the third grade. Lisa is on a first name basis with Carmen's mother, but sometimes to be mean she calls her Mrs. Bejarano. She wishes Carmen knew how to fight back.

Her lipgloss is the color of rubber gloves. She slides it over Carmen's open mouth. She wonders what it would feel like to slip her tongue inside.

Bear walks into a bar and rises up on hind legs to his full, considerable height. Fireworks explode and even though the DJ has cued up his secret weapon, the dance floor clears.

Carmen's mother invited herself. She tells Carmen she'll be her conscience, meaning she'll prevent her from ordering chili fries or cheese curds or the Moonglow specialty: tater tot nachos.

Bear lifts his snout and sniffs. There is no escaping the trash that is Carmen's mother.

The DJ flirts with all three of them. Carmen thinks he looks like Will Riker from Star Trek: Next Generation. He tells them the job is harder than it looks, that the cardinal sin of DJ-ing is clearing the dance floor.

Bear walks into a bar and even though Rock the Casbah's playing the dance floor clears.

Maybe they all rushed out to watch the fireworks. Bears find such displays confusing, like flashing lights and loud music and drunks falling off their barstools. It is not New Year's Eve nor is it the Fourth of July. Maybe it's a new thing, a Friday night thing at The Moonglow.

Lisa and Carmen escape to the ladies room. It's packed. Carmen's so wasted. All night, Lisa's been passing her Fireball shots under the table. Close your mouth, Lisa says. Blink. Carmen does not comply.

Lisa unscrews the cap of the lipgloss and slides it over Carmen's mouth. Lisa's lipgloss is the color of the rubber gloves she imagines Mrs. Bejarano uses to scrub the toilet. It calms her to think of this. Come closer, Lisa whispers. She hooks her finger in the belt loop of her friend's jeans.

Carmen's mother got her a FitBit for her sixteenth birthday. Carmen must walk ten-thousand steps before she is given her evening meal. Carmen walks five thousand steps to McDonald's and five thousand steps back. Her mother smells the Big Mac on her breath and punishes her with a three-day supervised fast.

Carmen's mother is pure, stinking, compostable trash.

Bear walks into a bar as fireworks detonate in a brilliant display worthy of such a fierce creature.

Bears do not need to reduce.

Bear kicks open the door to the ladies room all sweat and adrenaline as if he's jacked up on something. He is not a grizzly or a brown bear or a black bear. He is not mighty. He is, in fact, small and human and white. He raises his gun and shoots.

Lisa and Carmen are on the floor, lying face-to-face. Lisa hooks her finger in the belt loop of her friend's jeans, holds her breath, and pulls. When Carmen's body, the whole warm heft of it, falls onto hers, Lisa closes her eyes and waits.

JOY KATZ

Adopted

Many people say I'm no more your mother

than the cloud

          about the baby that distills a mirror

                to reflect its own slow effacement

About the baby at the wind's hand

               many people say

he looks a far sea moves

          like me in my ear

A Walk

My son walks along holding Xuan's hand. Xuan: younger, also adopted. I can see my son enjoys that he visually belongs with Xuan. A half-block away, they appear to be, or are, complete.

In one of the memoirs, a Korean adoptee moves from Kansas to Seoul, back with her birth mother. She fell in love with the fact that they have the same sneeze.

The head of my department—an adoptee—on learning I have an adopted son: "He's already angry about that. Just you wait."

"Why did my mother give me away?" he asks at dinner. The question. *How could anyone have given up such as you,* I say. *I can't know, but it must have been hard.* Then, a minute later: *Next time around you can have a different mom.* I don't say this, but almost do. He was whining for more dessert. How easy it is, at any moment, to send him spinning through the universe alone.

No. It is myself I almost cast off, every time, without him.

Does Xuan ever talk about his birthmother? I ask my friend Kath, on our walk. She falls backward onto a fence, spitting. She is enraged: "I am the mother. I am the *only* mother." Our kids are a full block ahead now, my son proudly holding the hand of her son.

Relax

You have come for massage. Need something rubbed away. Shut your eyes. Listen: a harvesting of sacred Hindu music for a loop of tragic minors. Tinkly piano, like a boy flicking water at you from a straw. Relax. Now the soundtrack is a girl weeping as the last blossoms fall from the tree. The spa therapist's press on your skin, intimate yet impersonal. Odor of sea buckthorn and arnica. Now the music is the scene where the young bride regains her memory and recognizes her true love. It is time to turn over on your back beneath the thin summer sheet. Recall the time a stranger ripped your shirt and shoved his hand down the front of your—

What music would you prefer to be touched to? We have available the sound of a small dog snoring. We have your mother shutting the silverware drawer. This music is meant to comfort; you must tell us very frankly what you need.

As Much as You Want

My shame is like a little flannel scrap safety-pinned inside my skirt hem. *I'm sorry. I'll do better*, I say when I harm you. I know not to go on, I know to stop talking. I can reach for my shame then and rub and rub and rub.

SARAH GRIDLEY

Whetting the Hoes

Some metal slicing against stone and water.
As you move
to the shapely barrier

of your final hour, see what little answerers
you'll be wanting
for the long fields of afterlife. Bright as wind

parting ribs from sand, the feeling both revealing and
relieving. The lost

green plant of you
between your teeth, behind
your dream of speaking.

L. S. KLATT

Snowflakes

Sometimes God opens his mouth, & moths fly out & hit
against the windshield, hoverers that melt
because of the defroster, & the spirit of the blower is

upon them. Moth No. 39 is celestial, as is 147. Headlights
magnify the white-winged borealis. You could drive
a truck through it, there is so much powder on the road; it drifts

like meal moths that winter in flour while eating up the Wonder
Bread of novices. The mouth has been under
attack for opening wide; you could blow a timeshare through it.

ERIN ADAIR-HODGES

Neighbors

Thin-lipped penitent who cruels the still dark morning,
have some mercy on your paper sisters
waking with heads full of sin, memories
and plans blinking themselves to ink and action.
Everyone just lives, somehow.
Even you, forgetful goat, boots before pants,
relentless clamberer of stairs.
Leave what you left in its space.
Your god forgives you already.
Instead of his judgment think of ours,
the women in the wall cackling through cracks,
our thinly spackled conspiracies.
We yellow and rouge, grow fat on moon.
We do not know your name but could.

DAVID DODD LEE

Poem for the Year Just Past

It's 62 degrees four days after Christmas
and I'm falling in love with a woman who
appears in a Lending Tree ad. The one time

I visited a circus I heard a male clown
complain to a female clown "I've got a fucking
eyelash in my eye again." I don't know. She

dabbed at it with a tissue or soft cloth.
I was older then, carrying a flask. I try
to imagine two clowns fucking and it's

possible to do. Like two dogs with human
bodies staring at each other through eye
holes, thrusting, not speaking. Another decade

is coming to a close, the return of the Swastika.
Everyone's trolling everyone else. I walk
where no one goes in winter, over paths

circling baseball diamonds, a tennis court
with a flimsy net sagging in the fog. I've
watched her commercial on YouTube more than

once at this point. Plus ones for AT&T,
Crest Toothpaste, an excerpt or three from
an obscure movie. Goodbye 2019, you heartbreaker.

MARK HALLIDAY

72nd Street Station

I'll be waiting for her at the 72nd Street station
just outside at the row of benches
waiting next to several individuals who are down and out
waiting there with less and less hope
as functional people with feasible plans pass by

I'll keep on waiting for her
while in another city at a corner table she frowns empathetically
at someone's manuscript and while I at that moment
in still another city catch the 38 bus
in order to fulfill feasible plans still my spirit will be
waiting for her just outside the 72nd Street station

—it's romantic, right? And I love romance, do I not?
But there is the dreariness of being stuck there waiting
so maybe I don't want it to be true unless
the persistence is crucial to the being of what feels like me
in a world where beauty is not a deniable imposition
as a light rain starts falling on 72nd Street
and imposes beauty on the stoical squares of slate.

Bios

ERIN ADAIR-HODGES' debut poetry collection *Let's All Die Happy* (U of Pittsburgh, 2017) won the Agnes Lynch Starrett Prize. Her work appears in *Boulevard, Crazyhorse, The Kenyon Review, Prairie Schooner,* and elsewhere. She teaches at the University of Central Missouri and edits *Pleiades*.

Fiction by **CARA BLUE ADAMS** appears in *American Short Fiction, Epoch, Granta,* and elsewhere. She has won the *Kenyon Review* Short Fiction Prize and the *Missouri Review*'s Peden Prize, as well as support from the Bread Loaf Writers' Conference, the Sewanee Writers' Conference, the Virginia Center for the Creative Arts, and the New York State Council on the Arts. She teaches at Seton Hall University and lives in Brooklyn.

DAN ALBERGOTTI is the author of *Millennial Teeth* (SIU, 2014) and *The Boatloads* (BOA, 2008) as well as two chapbooks from Unicorn Press: *Of Air and Earth* (2019) and *The Use of the World* (2013). His poems have appeared in *Crazyhorse, Five Points, The Southern Review, The Best American Poetry 2017,* two editions of *The Pushcart Prize,* and elsewhere. He teaches at Coastal Carolina University.

PAMELA ALEXANDER is the author of four poetry collections, most recently *Slow Fire* (Ausable, 2007). She taught for many years at MIT and Oberlin College, and now lives in Tucson, Arizona.

MEGAN ALPERT is the author of *The Animal at Your Side* (Airlie Press, 2020), which won the Airlie Prize. Her work has appeared or is forthcoming in *Crab Orchard Review, Glass: Poets Resist, Tinderbox Poetry Journal,* and elsewhere. As a journalist, she has reported for *The Atlantic, Foreign Policy, The Guardian,* and *Smithsonian.*

MESÁNDEL VIRTUSIO ARGUELLES is the author of 20 books, including most recently *Mujeres Publicas* (Balangay Productions, 2019) and bilingual editions (tr. Kristine Ong Muslim) *Walang Halong Biro* (De La Salle University Publishing House, 2018) and *Three Books* (Broken Sleep Books, forthcoming September 2020). A recipient of multiple national awards, Arguelles teaches at the De La Salle University in Manila. For more information, see page 209.

ROBERT ARCHAMBEAU's most recent book, *Poetry and Uselessness from Coleridge to Ashbery*, was published in 2020 by Routledge. A poet and critic of literature and art, his writing appears frequently in such journals as *Hudson Review* and *Hyperallergic*.

RUTH AWAD is the Lebanese-American author of *Set to Music a Wildfire* (Southern Indiana Review Press, 2017), which won the 2016 Michael Waters Poetry Prize and the 2018 Ohioana Book Award. With Rachel Mennies, she is co-editor of *The Familiar Wild: On Dogs and Poetry* (Sundress, 2020), and she has received two Ohio Arts Council Individual Excellence Awards and two Dorothy Sargent Rosenberg Poetry Prizes. Her work appears in *The Believer*, *The New Republic*, *Pleiades*, *Poetry*, and elsewhere. She lives in Columbus, Ohio.

Originally from St. Louis, **SARAH BARBER** lives in upstate New York, where she teaches at St. Lawrence University. Her poetry collections are *Country House* (Pleiades, 2018), which won the Pleiades Press Editors Prize, and *The Kissing Party* (National Poetry Review, 2010). Her poems appear in *Crazyhorse*, *Columbia Poetry Review*, *New Ohio Review*, *Poetry*, and elsewhere.

MICHAEL BAZZETT is the author of three collections of poetry: *The Interrogation* (Milkweed, 2017); *Our Lands Are Not So Different* (Horsethief, 2017); and *You Must Remember This* (Milkweed, 2014), which won the Linquist & Vennum Prize. His poems have appeared in *The American Poetry Review*, *The Sun*, *Threepenny Review*, *Tin House*, and elsewhere. His verse translation of the Mayan creation epic, *The Popol Vuh*, (Milkweed, 2018) was named "one of 2018's ten best books of poetry" by the *New York Times*. He lives in Minneapolis.

DESPY BOUTRIS' work has been published or is forthcoming in *American Literary Review*, *The American Poetry Review*, *Colorado Review*, *The Journal*, *Prairie Schooner*, and elsewhere. She teaches at the University of Houston, works as an assistant poetry editor for *Gulf Coast*, and serves as editor-in-chief of *The West Review*.

GERRI BRIGHTWELL is a British writer who lives in Alaska with her husband, fantasy writer Ian C. Esslemont, and their three sons. She is the author of the novels *Dead of Winter* (Salt, 2016), *The Dark Lantern* (Crown, 2008), and *Cold Country* (Duckworth, 2003). Her short work has appeared in such venues as *Alaska Quarterly Review*, *Redivider*, *Southwest Review*, *The Best American Mystery Stories 2017*, and *BBC Radio 4's Opening Lines*. She teaches at the University of Alaska, Fairbanks.

JENNIFER BROWN has held residencies at the Weymouth Center for the Arts and the Vermont Studio Center. In 2018 she won the Linda Flowers Literary Award from the North Carolina Humanities Council. Her essays and poems appear in *Atticus Review*, *Muse/A*, *North Carolina Literary Review*, *Stonecrop*, and elsewhere.

SARA BURNETT's chapbook is *Mother Tongue* (Dancing Girl, 2018), and her poems have appeared in *Barrow Street*, *The Cortland Review*, *Poet Lore*, the anthology *Bullets into Bells*, and elsewhere. She has received fellowships from the Bread Loaf Writers Conference and was a finalist for the 2019 Enoch Pratt Library Poetry Prize.

Born in El Fuerte, Sinaloa, in 1988, **CÉSAR CAÑEDO** won the 2019 Premio Bellas Artes de Poesía Aguascalientes for his book *Sigo escondiéndome detrás de mis ojos* (Fóndo de Cultura Económica, 2019, https://bit.ly/2M8dIzY). He teaches at the National Autonomous University of Mexico (UNAM).

VICTORIA CHANG's most recent books are *Obit* (Copper Canyon, 2020) and *Barbie Chang* (2018). The recipient of a 2017 Guggenheim Fellowship, she directs the MFA Program at Antioch Los Angeles.

HEDGIE CHOI is a fellow at the Michener Center for Writers in Austin, Texas.

ADAM CLAY's most recent book is *To Make Room for the Sea* (Milkweed, 2020). He directs the Center for Writers at the University of Southern Mississippi and edits *Mississippi Review*.

PETER COOLEY is the author of ten books of poetry, nine of them published by Carnegie Mellon, the most recent of which is *World Without Finishing*, 2018. He is Professor Emeritus of English at Tulane University, where he directed the creative writing program from 1975–2018. He currently serves as poetry editor of *Christianity and Literature*.

LISA FAY COUTLEY is the author of *tether* (Black Lawrence, 2020); *Errata* (Southern Illinois UP, 2015), winner of the Crab Orchard Series in Poetry Open Competition Award; and *In the Carnival of Breathing* (Black Lawrence, 2011), winner of the Black River Chapbook Competition. She is the recipient of a fellowship from the National Endowment for the Arts and teaches at the University of Nebraska at Omaha.

ROBIN DAVIDSON is the author of two chapbooks and the collection *Luminous Other* (Ashland Poetry, 2013), awarded the Richard Snyder Memorial Publication Prize. She has received a Fulbright professorship at Jagiellonian University in Kraków, Poland, and an NEA fellowship in translation. With Ewa Elżbieta Nowakowska she is co-translator of *the New Century: Poems from the Polish of Ewa Lipska* (Northwestern UP, 2009). She teaches as professor emeritus at the University of Houston-Downtown.

WHITNEY DeVOS is a writer, translator, and scholar currently based in Mexico City. Her translations have appeared in *The Acentos Review, Chicago Review, Full Stop*, and *Latin American Literature Today*; her translation of *Notes Toward a Pamphlet* by Sergio Chejfec appeared this year with Ugly Duckling Presse.

HILDE DOMIN (1909–2006) was a German Jewish poet, born in Cologne, who lived in Rome, England, and the Dominican Republic before returning to West Germany in 1954. For more information, see page 75.

MATT DONOVAN is the author of two collections of poetry—*Rapture & the Big Bam* (Tupelo, 2017) and *Vellum* (Mariner, 2007)—as well as the book of lyric essays, *A Cloud of Unusual Size and Shape* (Trinity UP, 2016). The recipient of a Whiting Award, a Rome Prize in Literature, a Pushcart Prize, a Creative Capital Grant, and an NEA Fellowship in Literature, Donovan serves as Director of the Poetry Center at Smith College.

ASA DRAKE is a Filipina American writer and public services librarian in Central Florida. Her most recent work is published or forthcoming in *Epiphany, Superstition Review*, and *Tupelo Quarterly*. She was a 2019 fellow for Idyllwild Arts Writers' Week and a finalist for Omnidawn's 2018 Chapbook Contest.

JEHANNE DUBROW is the author of seven poetry collections—most recently *American Samizdat* (Diode, 2019)—and a book of creative nonfiction, *throughsmoke: an essay in notes* (New Rivers, 2019). She teaches at the University of North Texas.

Originally from Cairo, **HAZEM FAHMY** is an MA student in Middle Eastern Studies and Film Studies at UT Austin. His chapbook *Red//Jild//Prayer* won the 2017 Diode Editions Chapbook Contest. A Kundiman and Watering Hole Fellow, Fahmy has published poetry in *Apogee, The Boston Review, The Offing*, and elsewhere.

The recipient of a 2020 Ragdale Foundation Fellowship, **KATHY FISH** has published five collections of flash fiction, most recently *Wild Life: Collected Works from 2003–2018* (Matter, 2018). She teaches in the Mile-High MFA at Regis University.

AIDAN FORSTER is the author of *Wrong June* (Honeysuckle, 2020) and *Exit Pastoral* (YesYes, 2019). His work appears in *Best New Poets 2017*, *Columbia Poetry Review*, *Ninth Letter*, *Tin House*, and elsewhere. He studies Literary Arts and Public Health at Brown University.

GUY GOFFETTE is the author of ten poetry collections from Editions Gallimard, most recently *Pain Perdu* (2020), as well as collections and chapbooks from other presses, memoirs, a novel, and idiosyncratic critical-biographical books about Verlaine, Bonnard, and Auden. *Charlestown Blues*, a bilingual collection of his poems and Marilyn Hacker's translations, was published by Princeton UP in 2007. He lives in Paris. For more information, see page 241.

A former Wallace Stegner Fellow, **JP GRASSER** is a PhD candidate at the University of Utah, where he edits *Quarterly West*.

SARAH GRIDLEY teaches at Case Western Reserve University in Cleveland, Ohio. She is the author of *Insofar* (New Issues, 2020), *Loom* (Omnidawn, 2013), *Green is the Orator* (U of California, 2010), and *Weather Eye Open* (2005).

RYAN HABERMEYER teaches creative writing and literature at Salisbury University. He is the author of the prize-winning collection of short stories, *The Science of Lost Futures* (BOA, 2018).

MARILYN HACKER is the author of fourteen poetry books, including *Blazons* (Carcanet, 2019) and *A Stranger's Mirror: New and Selected Poems, 1004–2014* (W. W. Norton, 2015), as well as the essay collection *Unauthorized Voices* (U of Michigan, 2010). Her sixteen translations of French and Francophone poets include Samira Negrouche's *The Olive Trees' Jazz* (Pleiades, 2020), and Emmanuel Moses' *Preludes and Fuges* (Oberlin, 2016). She lives in Paris.

MARK HALLIDAY teaches at Ohio University. His seventh book of poems *Losers Dream On* was published in 2018 by the University of Chicago Press.

HENRY ISRAELI's most recent poetry collections are *Our Age of Anxiety* (White Pine, 2019), which won the White Pine Press Prize, and *god's breath hovering across the waters* (Four Way, 2016). The recipient of fellowships from the NEA and the Canada Council on the Arts, he teaches at *Drexel University* and is founder and editor of Saturnalia Books.

Born in the Philippines, **JANINE JOSEPH** is the author of *Driving Without a License* (Alice James, 2016), winner of the Kundiman Poetry Prize. Her writing appears in *The Atlantic*, *The Georgia Review*, *Orion Magazine*, *Pleiades*, and elsewhere. Her libretti for the Houston Grand Opera/HGOco include *In Our Care*, *What Wings They Were*, *"On This Muddy Water,"* and *From My Mother's Mother*. A co-organizer for Undocupoets and a MacDowell Fellow, Joseph teaches at Oklahoma State University.

W. TODD KANEKO is the author of the poetry books *This Is How the Bone Sings* (Black Lawrence, 2020) and *The Dead Wrestler Elegies* (Curbside Splendor, 2014), as well as co-author of *Poetry: A Writer's Guide and Anthology* (Bloomsbury Academic, 2018). He is a Kundiman fellow and teaches at Grand Valley State University in Grand Rapids, Michigan.

J. KATES is a poet and literary translator who lives in Fitzwilliam, New Hampshire.

JOY KATZ is the author of three poetry collections—most recently *All You Do Is Perceive* (Four Way, 2013)—and two chapbooks. Her new manuscript, *The Color Cure*, documents every minute of whiteness in her life. A past NEA and Stegner fellow, she collaborates in the activist art collective IfYouReallyLoveMe, based in Pittsburgh, and teaches in Carlow University's Madwomen in the Attic writing workshops for women.

Originally from Glens Falls, New York, **MATTHEW KELSEY** lives in Chicago. His poems appear in *Beloit Poetry Journal*, *Colorado Review*, *Poetry Northwest*, *Best New Poets*, and elsewhere. He has received scholarships from the Bread Loaf Writers' Conference and the Sewanee Writers' Conference, a teaching fellowship from the Kenyon Review Young Writers Program, and an Idyllwild Arts Writers Week Fellowship.

DAVID KIRBY's most recent poetry collections are *More Than This* (LSU, 2019) and *Get Up, Please* (2016). The recipient of NEA and Guggenheim Fellowships, he teaches at Florida State University.

L. S. KLATT is the author of four poetry collections, including his latest, *The Wilderness After Which* (Seismicity, 2017). New poems of his appear in *Carolina Quarterly, Image, The Iowa Review, New American Writing,* and *The Southern Review,* and his essay "Blue Buzz, Blue Guitar: Wallace Stevens and the Poetics of Noisemaking" was published recently in *The Georgia Review.*

YUSEF KOMUNYAKAA has won, among many awards, the Wallace Stevens Award, the Ruth Lilly Poetry Prize, the Kingsley Tufts Poetry Award, and the Pulitzer Prize. *Everyday Mojo Songs of Earth: New and Selected Poems, 2001–2021* is forthcoming from FSG in 2021.

DIMITRA KOTOULA is a Greek poet and archaeologist. Poems from her (thus far) two poetry collections have been translated into thirteen languages. For more information, see page 189.

JENNIFER KRONOVET is the author of two poetry collections: *The Wug Test* (Ecco, 2017), which won the National Poetry Series, and *Awayward* (BOA, 2009). As Jennifer Stern, she co-translated *Empty Chairs,* poems of Chinese Writer Liu Xia. She edits Circumference Books.

MICHAEL LAVERS is the author of *After Earth* (U of Tampa, 2019). His poems have appeared in *Crazyhorse, The Georgia Review, 32 Poems, TriQuarterly, Best New Poets,* and elsewhere. He teaches at Brigham Young University.

DAVID DODD LEE is the author of nine full-length books of poems, most recently *And Others, Vaguer Presences: A Book of Ashbery Erasure Poems* (BlazeVOX, 2016) and *Animalities* (Four Way, 2014). His fiction has appeared in *Green Mountains Review, New World Writing, Sou'wester, Willow Springs,* and elsewhere. In 2016 he began making sculpture, most of which he installs surreptitiously on various public lands. *Unlucky Animals,* a book of collages, photographs, poems, erasures, and dictionary sonnets, is scheduled for publication in 2020 from Wolfson Press.

HAILEY LEITHAUSER is the author of the poetry collections *Saint Worm* (Able Muse, 2019) and *Swoop* (Graywolf, 2013). Her recent poems appear in *Agni, Birmingham Poetry Review, The Hopkins Review, Plume,* and elsewhere.

EWA LIPSKA, born in 1945 in Kraków, Poland, is the author of over 30 volumes of poetry, and her poems have been translated into more than 15 languages. For more information, see page 17.

MAXIM LOSKUTOFF is the author of *Ruthie Fear* (W. W. Norton 2020) and *Come West and See* (2018). His stories and essays have appeared in numerous publications, including the *Chicago Tribune*, *New York Times*, *Ploughshares*, and the *Southern Review*. He lives in western Montana.

RANDALL MANN is the author of five books of poems, most recently *Proprietary* (Persea, 2017), which was a finalist for the Northern California Book Award and the Lambda Literary Award, and the forthcoming *A Better Life* (2021). His book of criticism is *The Illusion of Intimacy: On Poetry* (Diode, 2019). He lives in San Francisco.

MICHAEL MARK's poetry has been published or forthcoming in *Alaska Quarterly Review*, *Michigan Quarterly Review*, *Pleiades*, *The New York Times*, and elsewhere. He is the author of two books of stories, *Toba* (Atheneum, 1984) and *At the Hands of a Thief* (1985).

LAREN McCLUNG is the author of a collection of poems, *Between Here and Monkey Mountain* (Sheep Meadow, 2012), and editor of the anthology *Inheriting the War: Poetry and Prose by Descendants of Vietnam Veterans and Refugees* (W. W. Norton, 2017). Her poems have appeared in *Boston Review*, *Harvard Review*, *Massachusetts Review*, *Poetry*, and elsewhere. She teaches at New York University.

KATHLEEN McGOOKEY has published four books of prose poems and three chap-books, most recently *Instructions for My Imposter* (Press 53) and *Nineteen Letters* (BatCat Press). She has also translated *We'll See*, a collection of French poet Georges Go-deau's prose poems. Her work has appeared in *Crazyhorse*, *Field*, *Ploughshares*, *Prairie Schooner*, and elsewhere, and she has received grants from the French Ministry of Foreign Affairs and the Sustainable Arts Foundation.

PABLO MEDINA is the author of nineteen books of fiction, nonfiction, poetry, and translation. *The Foreigner's Song: New and Selected Poems* is forthcoming in the fall of 2020. He is the recipient of fellowships from the NEA, the Rockefeller Foundation, and the John Simon Guggenheim Foundation, among others. He is currently on fac-ulty at the Warren Wilson College MFA Program for Writers. He lives in Vermont.

SARA MICHAS-MARTIN is the author of *Gray Matter*, winner of the Poets Out Loud Prize and nominated for a Colorado Book Award. Her essays and poems have appeared in *The American Poetry Review*, *The Believer*, *Best New Poets*, *Denver Quarterly*, *jubi-lat*, and elsewhere. She is a Jones Lecturer in the Creative Writing Program at Stanford University.

MOON BO YOUNG was born in Jeju, South Korea, in 1992, and is a graduate of Korea University. In 2016 she won the Joong Ang New Writers Award, and her poetry collection *Pillar of Books* won the 36th Kim Soo-young Literary Award.

ERÍN MOURE's latest book is *The Elements* (Anansi, 2019). Her latest translations are a sequence of Argentinian poet Juan Gelman's "translations" of John Wendell, *Sleepless Nights Under Capitalism* (Eulalia, 2020) and, from the Galician of Uxío Novoneyra, *The Uplands, Book of the Courel* (Veliz, 2020).

NIHAL MUBARAK is a poet and short story writer who recently completed an MFA at Emerson College.

Work by **CHRISTOPHER BREAN MURRAY** appears in *Cimarron Review, Conduit, Grist, Poet Lore*, and elsewhere. He is a recent graduate of the PhD program in Writing and Literature the University of Houston.

KRISTINE ONG MUSLIM is the author of nine books, including the fiction collections *The Drone Outside* (Eibonvale, 2017), *Butterfly Dream* (Snuggly, 2016), and *Age of Blight* (Unnamed, 2016). She is co-editor of two anthologies—the British Fantasy Award-winning *People of Colo(u)r Destroy Science Fiction* and *Sigwa: Climate Fiction Anthology from the Philippines* (Polytechnic University of the Philippines, 2020). Her stories appear in *Conjunctions, Tin House, World Literature Today*, and elsewhere.

MARIA NAZOS' poetry is published in *The Florida Review, The New Yorker, The Tampa Review, TriQuarterly*, and elsewhere. Her chapbook-length translations, including that of Dimitra Kotoula, entitled *This Slow Horizon Behind Me That Breathes*, have appeared in *The Mid-American Review*.

MARK NEELY is the author of *Dirty Bomb* (2015) and *Beasts of the Hill* (2012), both from Oberlin College Press. His awards include an NEA Poetry Fellowship, an Indiana Individual Artist grant, and the FIELD Poetry Prize. He teaches at Ball State University and is a senior editor at *River Teeth: A Journal of Nonfiction Narrative*.

EWA ELŻBIETA NOWAKOWSKA is a poet and translator (of, among others, Alice Munroe, Thomas Merton, and Elif Shafak). A graduateof Jagiellonian University's Institute of English Philology, she is the author of seven poetry volumes and a collection of stories. She has received several literary awards in Poland, including the Krzysztof Kamil Baczyński Literary Prize and Krakow's Book of the Month Prize for her collection *Trzy ołówki*.

Writing by **CAROLYN OLIVER** has appeared in *Beloit Poetry Journal*, *The Cincinnati Review*, *Indiana Review*, and *Tin House Online*, and she recently won the Goldstein Poetry Prize from *Michigan Quarterly Review*. She lives in Massachusetts with her family.

MATTHEW OLZMANN is the author of two collections of poems, *Contradictions in the Design* (2016) and *Mezzanines* (2013), both from Alice James Books. His third book of poems, *Constellation Route*, is forthcoming in January 2022. He teaches at Dartmouth College and in the MFA Program for Writers at Warren Wilson College.

Galician (Spain), poet **CHUS PATO** has received the Spanish Critics' Prize and the Losada Diéguez Prize, and she was named 2013 Author of the Year by the Galician Booksellers' Association, In 2015, her work was recorded for the sound archives of the Woodberry Poetry Room (Harvard). All five of the books in her pentalogy *Décrua* have been published in English translation. For more information, see page 155.

CARL PHILLIPS' most recent book is *Pale Colors in a Tall Field* (FSG, 2020). Phillips teaches at Washington University in St. Louis.

CAROLINE PLASKET's work has been published or is forthcoming in *Atticus Review*, *The Cortland Review*, *The Laurel Review*, *Orange Blossom Review*, *Spoon River Poetry Review*, and elsewhere. She was a fall 2016 mentee in the AWP Writer to Writer Program. She lives in the Cincinnati area.

LOTTE MITCHELL REFORD is a London-based poet, writer, and editor. Her work appears in *Cosmonauts Avenue*, *Hobart*, *The Moth*, *SPAM*, and elsewhere. Her chapbook *and we were so far from the sea of course the hermit crabs were dead* is forthcoming from Broken Sleep Books in 2021.

MAXINE SCATES' fourth book of poetry, *My Wilderness*, is forthcoming from the University of Pittsburgh Press in the fall of 2021. Her poems have been widely published in such journals as *Agni*, *The American Poetry Review*, *The New England Review*, *The New Yorker*, *Ploughshares*, and elsewhere, and have received, among other awards, the Starrett Prize, the Oregon Book Award for Poetry, and two Pushcart Prizes.

STEVEN D. SCHROEDER's second book, *The Royal Nonesuch* (Spark Wheel, 2013), won the Devil's Kitchen Reading Award from Southern Illinois University. His poetry appears recently in *The Cincinnati Review*, *Diagram*, *Michigan Quarterly Review*, and elsewhere. He works as a creative content manager for a financial marketing agency in St. Louis.

CINDY SCHUSTER is a poet and translator. She is co-translator of the anthology *Cubana: Contemporary Fiction by Cuban Women* (Beacon Press, 1998). Her translations of fiction and poetry have appeared in *The American Voice, Exquisite Corpse, Poetry International, Words Without Borders,* and elsewhere. She has been awarded a Translation Fellowship from the National Endowment for the Arts for her translation of a collection of short stories by Rodolfo Walsh.

MAUREEN SEATON has authored twenty-one poetry collections, both solo and collaborative—most recently, *Sweet World* (CavanKerry, 2019) and *Fisher* (Black Lawrence, 2018). Her awards include the Iowa Prize, two Lambda Literary Awards, the Audre Lorde Award, the Sentence Book Award (with Neil de la Flor), an NEA fellowship, and a Pushcart Prize. Seaton teaches at the University of Miami.

JOHN SKOYLES' most recent book is *Driven* (Madhad, 2019), a memoir in travelogue form. His books of poems include *Inside Job* (Carnegie Mellon, 2016) and *Suddenly It's Evening: Selected Poems* (2016). He is the poetry editor of *Ploughshares.*

ELEANOR STANFORD is the author of three books of poetry: *The Imaginal Marriage* (2018), *Bartram's Garden* (2015), and *The Book of Sleep* (2008), all from Carnegie Mellon UP. Her work has appeared in *Iowa Review, The Kenyon Review, Ploughshares, Poetry,* and elsewhere. She was a 2014/2016 Fulbright fellow to Brazil, where she researched and wrote about traditional midwifery, and a 2018 NEA fellow in poetry. She lives in the Philadelphia area.

Guggenheim fellow **TERESE SVOBODA** is the author of 18 books, most recently the story collection *Great American Desert* (Mad Creek, 2019), the biography *Anything That Burns You: A Portrait of Lola Ridge, Radical Poet* (Schaffner, 2016), and the forthcoming poetry collection *Theatrix: Play Poems* (Anhinga, 2021).

CRAIG MORGAN TEICHER is the author of several books, most recently the essay collection *We Begin in Gladness: How Poets Progress* (Graywolf, 2018) and *The Trembling Answers* (BOA, 2017), which won the Lenore Marshall Poetry Prize from the Academy of American Poets. His next book will be out from BOA in Spring 2021.

SETH BRADY TUCKER directs the Longleaf Writers Conference and teaches at the Lighthouse Writer's Workshop and at the Colorado School of Mines. His second book, *We Deserve the Gods We Ask For* (2014), won the Gival Press Poetry Award and the Eric Hoffer Book Award. His first book, *Mormon Boy* (2012), won the Elixir Press Editor's Prize.

CLAIRE WAHMANHOLM is the author of *Redmouth* (Tinderbox, 2019); *Wilder* (Milkweed, 2018), which won the Lindquist & Vennum Prize; and *Night Vision* (New Michigan, 2017), which won New Michigan Press/*DIAGRAM* chapbook contest. Her poems appear in *Beloit Poetry Journal*, *RHINO*, *32 Poems*, *West Branch*, and elsewhere. She lives in the Twin Cities.

G. C. WALDREP is the author, most recently, of *feast gently* (Tupelo, 2018), winner of the William Carlos Williams Award from the Poetry Society of America, and the long poem *Testament* (BOA Editions, 2015). *The Earliest Witnesses* is due out in January 2021 from Tupelo in the US and Carcanet in the UK. Waldrep lives in Lewisburg, Pennsylvania, where he teaches at Bucknell University and edits the journal *West Branch*.

Renowned as a canonical writer in Argentina, **RODOLFO WALSH** (1927-1977) is recognized for his compelling fiction, his investigative journalism, his experimentation with genre, and his stylistic innovations. An exemplar of the ideal of the politically committed intellectual, he was assassinated by soldiers from the Navy School of Engineers in 1977, one day after making public his famous "Open Letter from a Writer to the Military Junta," which denounced the crimes of the dictatorship. For more information, see page 169.

BRIAN PHILLIP WHALEN's debut collection of fiction, *Semiotic Love [Stories]*, will be released in early 2021 by Awst Press. His work has appeared in *Creative Nonfiction*, *The Los Angeles Review*, *North American Review*, *The Southern Review*, the *Flash Nonfiction Food* anthology, and elsewhere. He teaches at the University of Alabama.

KATHLEEN WINTER's poetry collections are *Transformer* (Word Works, 2020); *I will not kick my friends* (Elixir, 2018), which won the Elixir Poetry Prize; and *Nostalgia for the Criminal Past* (2012), which won the Texas Institute of Letters Bob Bush Award. Her poems have appeared in *The New Republic*, *New Statesman*, *Poetry London*, *Tin House*, and elsewhere. She has received fellowships from the Sewanee Writers' Conference, the Dora Maar House, the James Merrill House, and the Dobie Paisano Ranch.

Required Reading

(issue 31&2)

(Each issue we ask that our contributors recommend up to three recent titles. What follows is the list generated by the writers in this issue.)

Hanif Abdurraqib, *Go Ahead into the Rain: Notes to A Tribe Called Quest* (Hazem Fahmy)

Samuel Ace, *Our Weather Our Sea* (Maureen Seaton)

Chantel Acevedo, *Muse Squad: The Cassandra Curse* (Maureen Seaton)

Nana Kwame Adjei-Brenyah, *Friday Black* (Nihal Mubarak, Brian Phillip Whalen)

Zaina Alsous, *A Theory of Birds* (Ruth Awad)

Eunice Andrada, *Flood Damages* (Kristine Ong Muslim)

Jessica Anthony, *Enter the Aardvark* (Terese Svoboda)

Emilio Araúxo, *Libro Da Ribeira Sacra* (Erín Moure)

Paul Auster, *4321* (David Kirby)

Oana Avasilichioaei, *Eight Track* (Erín Moure)

Cameron Awkward-Rich, *Dispatch* (Randall Mann)

Taneum Bambrick, *Vantage* (Randall Mann)

Zeina Hashem Beck, *Louder Than Hearts* (Marilyn Hacker)

Jeanne Benameur, *The Child Who*, trans. Bill Johnston (Robin Davidson)

Oliver Baez Bendorf, *Advantages of Being Evergreen* (Randall Mann)

Marie-Helene Bertino, *Parakeet* (Adam Clay)

Reginald Dwayne Betts, *Felon* (Ruth Awad, Maxine Scates)

Mark Bibbins, *13th Balloon* (Henry Israeli)

Sarah Blake, *Naamah* (Eleanor Stanford)

Jaswinder Bolina, *Of Color* (Maureen Seaton)

Kate Briggs, *This Little Art* (Pablo Medina)

Traci Brimhall, *Come the Slumberless to the Land of Nod* (Caroline Plasket)

Kevin Brockmeier, *A Few Seconds of Radiant Filmstrip: A Memoir of Seventh Grade* (Kathleen McGookey)

Jericho Brown, *The Tradition* (Sara Burnett, Seth Brady Tucker)

Octavia E. Butler, *Lilith's Brood* (Craig Morgan Teicher)

Kayleb Rae Candrilli, *All the Gay Saints* (Despy Boutris)

Rachel Carson, *The Sea Around Us* (Sarah Gridley)

Marcelo Hernandez Castillo, *Children of the Land* (Sarah Gridley)

Jody Chan, *haunt* (Despy Boutris)

Victoria Chang, *Obit* (Sara Michas-Martin, G. C. Waldrep)

Don Mee Choi, *DMZ Colony* (Jennifer Kronovet)

Franny Choi, *Soft Science* (Caroline Plasket)

Thomas A. Clark, *Farm by the Shore* (Sarah Gridley)

Tiana Clark, *I Can't Talk About the Trees Without the Blood* (Mark Neely)

Aaron Coleman, *Threat Come Close* (Steven D. Schroeder)

Wanda Coleman, *Wicked Enchantment: Selected Poems*, ed. Terrance Hayes (Sarah Barber)

Martha Collins, *Because What Else Could I Do* (Pamela Alexander, Cindy Schuster)

Eduardo C. Corral, *Guillotine* (Maria Nazos)

Cynthia Cruz, *Dregs* (Aidan Forster)

Rachel Cusk, *Arlington Park* (Peter Cooley)

Angela Y. Davis, *Are Prisons Obsolete?* (Ruth Awad)

Roger Deakin, *Waterlog: A Swimmer's Journey Through Britain* (Sarah Barber)

Giorgio de Chirico, *Geometry of Shadows*, trans. Stefania Heim (Jennifer Kronovet)

Luca Del Baldo, *The Visionary Academy of Ocular Mentality* (Robert Archambeau)

Juli Delgado Lopera, *Fiebre Tropical* (Joy Katz)

Carl Dennis, *Night School* (Michael Lavers)

Toi Derricotte, *I: New and Selected Poems* (Yusef Komunyakaa)

Natalie Diaz, *Postcolonial Love Poem* (Victoria Chang, Laren McClung, Maria Nazos, Maxine Scates)

Juditha Dowd, *Audobon's Sparrow: A Biography-in-Poems* (Pamela Alexander)

Camille T. Dungy, *Trophic Cascade.* (Carolyn Oliver)

Marcella Durand, *The Prospect* (Joy Katz)

Ma-I Saffron Germaine Eligado Entico, *My Name is Agung* (Kristine Ong Muslim)

Jill Alexander Essbaum, *Would-Land* (Steven D. Schroeder)

Brian Evenson, *Song for the Unraveling of the World* (Kristine Ong Muslim)

Joe Fletcher, *The Hatch* (Christopher Brean Murray)

Carolyn Forché, *In the Lateness of the World* (Peter Cooley, Robin Davidson)

Meg Freitag, *Edith* (Caroline Plasket)

Romina Freschi, *Echo of the Park*, trans. Jeannine Marie Pitas (Joy Katz)

Maria Gainza, *Optic Nerve*, trans. Thomas Bunstead (Cara Blue Adams)

Martin Gayford, *A Bigger Message: Conversations with David Hockney* (L. S. Klatt)

Masha Gessen, *The Future Is History: How Totalitarianism Reclaimed Russia* (Jehanne Dubrow)

Megan Giddings, *Lakewood* (Kathy Fish)

Jennifer Givhan, *Trinity Sight* (Megan Alpert)

Renee Gladman, *Houses of Ravicka* (Jennifer Kronovet)

Joseph Goosey, *Parade of Malfeasance* (David Dodd Lee)

Kathleen Graber, *The River Twice* (Maxine Scates)

Garth Greenwell, *What Belongs to You* (Cara Blue Adams)

JP Gritton, *Wyoming* (Christopher Brean Murray)

Nathalie Handal, *Life in a Country Album* (Yusef Komunyakaa)

Terrance Hayes, *American Sonnets for My Past and Future Assassin* (Maria Nazos)

Terrance Hayes, *To Float in the Space Between: A Life and Work in Conversation with the Life and Work of Etheridge Knight* (Matthew Kelsey)

Rebecca Hazelton, *Gloss* (Lisa Fay Coutley)

Yuri Herrera, *Signs Preceding the End of the World*, trans. Lisa Dillman (Michael Bazzett)

Tony Hoagland, *Priest Turned Therapist Treats Fear of God* (Mark Halliday)

Lily Hoang, *A Bestiary* (Ryan Habermeyer)

Homer, *The Odyssey*, trans. Emily Wilson (Mark Neely)

Cathy Park Hong, *Minor Feelings* (Victoria Chang)

Erin Hoover, *Barnburner* (Megan Alpert)

Fanny Howe, *Love and I* (David Dodd Lee)

Chris Hutchinson, *In the Vicinity of Riches* (Christopher Brean Murray)

Su Hwang, *Bodega* (W. Todd Kaneko)

Kirstin Innes, *Scabby Queen* (Lotte Mitchell Reford)

Mira Jacob, *Good Talk: A Memoir in Conversations* (Carl Phillips)

Jessica Jacobs, *Take Me with You, Wherever You're Going* (Matthew Olzmann)

Didi Jackson, *Moon Jar* (Laren McClung)

Mitchell S. Jackson, *Survival Math: Notes on an All-American Family* (Jennifer Brown)

Honorée Fanonne Jeffers, *The Age of Phillis* (Carl Phillips)

Marlin M. Jenkins, *Capable Monsters* (W. Todd Kaneko)

Amaud Jamaul Johnson, *Imperial Liquor* (Matthew Olzmann)

Tayari Jones, *An American Marriage* (Nihal Mubarak)

Ilya Kaminsky, *Deaf Republic* (Sara Burnett, Hedgie Choi, Lisa Fay Coutley, Robin Davidson, Hazem Fahmy, Carolyn Oliver)

Mimi Khalvati, *Afterwardness* (Marilyn Hacker)

Katie Kitamura, *A Separation* (Gerri Brightwell)

John Koethe, *Walking Backwards* (Michael Lavers)

E. J. Koh, *The Magical Language of Others* (Victoria Chang)

Priya Krishna, *Indian-ish: Recipes and Antics from a Modern American Family* (Sarah Barber)

Keetje Kuipers, *All Its Charms* (Dan Albergotti)

R. O. Kwon, *The Incendiaries* (Hazem Fahmy)

Michael Lavers, *After Earth* (Claire Wahmanholm)

Dorianne Laux, *Only As the Day Is Long: New and Selected Poems* (Mark Halliday, Henry Israeli)

Paul Lisicky, *Later: My Life at the Edge of the World* (John Skoyles)

Valeria Luiselli, *Lost Children Archive* (Cindy Schuster)

Lynn Lurie, *Museum of Stones* (Terese Svoboda)

Robert Macfarlane, *Landmarks (Landscapes)* (David Kirby)

Carmen Maria Machado, *In the Dream House* (Despy Boutris, Carolyn Oliver)

Sara Majka, *Cities I've Never Lived In* (Cara Blue Adams)

Megha Majumdar, *A Burning* (Maxim Loskutoff)

Khaled Mattawa, *Fugitive Atlas* (Marilyn Hacker)

John Matthias, *Acoustic Shadows* (Robert Archambeau)

Shane McCrae, *In the Language of My Captor* (Mark Neely)

Shane McCrae, *Sometimes I Never Suffered* (G. C. Waldrep)

Will McGrath, *Everything Lost Is Found Again: Four Seasons in Lesotho* (Michael Bazzett)

Erika Meitner, *Holy Moly Carry Me* (Dan Albergotti, Matt Donovan)

Daniel Mendelsohn, *An Odyssey: A Father, a Son, and an Epic* (Matt Donovan)

Lydia Millet, *A Children's Bible* (Terese Svoboda)

Chelsey Minnis, *Baby, I Don't Care* (David Dodd Lee)

Anis Mojgani, *In the Pockets of Small Gods* (Jennifer Brown)

Jenny Molberg, *Refusal* (Erin Adair-Hodges, Kathleen Winter)

Matt Morton, *Improvisation Without Accompaniment* (JP Grasser)

Otessa Moshfegh, *My Year of Rest and Relaxation* (Hedgie Choi)

John Murillo, *Kontemporary Amerikan Poetry* (Henry Israeli, Janine Joseph, Laren McClung)

Serge Neptune, *These Queer Merboys* (Lotte Mitchell Reford)

Amy Newman, *On This Day in Poetry History* (David Kirby)

Catherine Newman, *Catastrophic Happiness: Finding Joy in Childhood's Messy Years* (Kathleen McGookey)

Diana Khoi Nguyen, *Ghost of* (Kathleen Winter)

Chessy Normile, *Great Exodus, Great Wall, Great Party* (Hedgie Choi)

Naomi Novik, *Spinning Silver* (Nihal Mubarak)

Kathryn Nuernberger, *Rue* (Erin Adair-Hodges)

Miller Oberman, *The Unstill Ones* (Hailey Leithauser)

Jenny Offill, *Department of Speculation* (Gerri Brightwell)

Yoko Ogawa, *The Memory Police*, trans. Stephen Snyder (Michael Bazzett)

Peter Orner, *Am I Alone Here? Notes on Living to Read and Reading to Live* (Brian Phillip Whalen)

Jill Osier, *The Solace Is Not the Lullaby* (John Skoyles)

Ed Pavlic, *Let It Be Broke* (Yusef Komunyakaa)

Mark Peterson, *The City-State of Boston: The Rise and Fall of an Atlantic Power, 1630–1865* (J. Kates)

Kiki Petrosino, *White Blood: A Lyric of Virginia* (L. S. Klatt)

Hai-Dang Phan, *Reenactments: Poems & Translations* (Matthew Kelsey)

Julia Phillips, *Disappearing Earth* (Maxim Loskutoff)

Andrea Pitzer, *One Long Night: A Global History of Concentration Camps* (Jehanne Dubrow)

John Poch, *Texases* (Kathleen Winter)

Michael Prior, *Burning Province* (Claire Wahmanholm)

Khadijah Queen, *I'm So Fine: A List of Famous Men & What I Had On* (Lisa Fay Coutley, Sara Michas-Martin)

Ed. Alice Quinn, *Together in a Sudden Strangeness: American Poets Respond to the Pandemic* (Peter Cooley)

Shivanee Ramlochan, *Everyone Knows I Am a Haunting* (Matthew Olzmann)

Paisley Rekdal, *Nightingale* (Janine Joseph)

Barbara Jane Reyes, *Letters to a Young Brown Girl* (Asa Drake)

Legna Rodríguez Iglesias, *Miami Century Fox*, trans. Eduardo Aparicio (Pablo Medina)

Reina María Rodríguez, *The Winter Garden Photograph*, trans. Kristin Dykstra
  (G. C. Waldrep)

Matthew Rohrer, *The Sky Contains the Plans* (Sara Michas-Martin)

Stefene Russell, *47 Incantatory Essays* (Steven D. Schroeder)

Jon Savage, *This searing light, the sun and everything else: Joy Division: The Oral History*
  (Dan Albergotti)

Edward Schwarzschild, *In Security* (Brian Phillip Whalen)

David Shariatmadari, *Don't Believe a Word: The Surprising Truth About Language*
  (Hailey Leithauser)

Prageeta Sharma, *Grief Sequence* (Joy Katz)

Brenda Shaughnessy, *The Octopus Museum* (Matthew Kelsey)

Martha Silano, *Gravity Assist* (Hailey Leithauser)

Johanna Skibsrud, *The Nothing That Is: Essays on Art, Literature, and Being* (Erín Moure)

John Skoyles, *Driven* (Pablo Medina)

Christopher Slatsky, *The Immeasurable Corpse of Nature* (Kristine Ong Muslim)

Carmen Giménez Smith, *Be Recorder* (Megan Alpert)

Katy Simpson Smith, *The Everlasting* (Adam Clay)

Patricia Smith, *Incendiary Art* (Jennifer Brown)

Timothy Snyder, *On Tyranny: Twenty Lessons from the Twentieth Century*
  (Jehanne Dubrow)

Amber Sparks, *And I Do Not Forgive You: Stories and Other Revenges* (Kathy Fish)

Patrick Syme, illust. Abraham Gottlob Werner, *Werner's Nomenclature of Colours:
  Adapted to Azoology, Botany, Chemistry, Mineralogy, Anatomy, and the Arts* (Janine Joseph)

Rebecca Tamas, *WITCH* (Lotte Mitchell Reford)

Brandon Taylor, *Real Life* (Erin Adair-Hodges)

Brian Teare, *Doomstead Days* (Aidan Forster)

Christina Thompson, *Sea People: The Puzzle of Polynesia* (J. Kates)

Olga Tokarczuk, *Drive Your Plow Over the Bones of the Dead*, trans. Antonia Lloyd-Jones
  (Gerri Brightwell)

Olga Tokarczuk, *Flights*, trans. Jennifer Croft (Ryan Habermeyer)

John Trimbur, *Grassroots Literacy and the Written Record: A Textual History of Asbestos Activism in South Africa* (John Skoyles)

Brian Turner, *My Life as a Foreign Country* (Seth Brady Tucker)

Asiya Wadud, *Crosslight for Youngbird* (Joy Katz)

Asiya Wadud, *Syncope* (Claire Wahmanholm)

Jesmyn Ward, *Sing, Unburied, Sing* (Sara Burnett, Seth Brady Tucker)

Claire Wahmanholm, *Redmouth* (Michael Lavers)

Kary Wayson, *The Slip* (Carl Phillips)

Colson Whitehead, *The Nickel Boys* (Matt Donovan)

Frank B. Wilderson III, *Afropessimism* (Aidan Forster)

Peter Wohlleben, *The Hidden Life of Trees: What They Feel, How They Communicate— Discoveries from a Secret World* (L. S. Klatt)

Jia Lynn Yang, *One Mighty and Irresistible Tide: The Epic Struggle Over American Immigration, 1924–1965* (Asa Drake)

John Yau, *Foreign Sounds or Sounds Foreign* (Robert Archambeau)

Jihyun Yun, *Some Are Always Hungry* (W. Todd Kaneko)

Michael Zadoorian, *Beautiful Music* (Kathleen McGookey)

Michael Zapata, *The Lost Book of Adana Moreau* (Maxim Loskutoff)

The Copper Nickel Editors' Prizes

(est. 2015)

(Two $500 prizes are awarded to the "most exciting work" published
in each issue, as determined by a vote of the *Copper Nickel* staff)

Past Winners

spring 2020 (issue 30)

Andrea Cohen, poetry
Maureen Langloss, prose

fall 2019 (issue 29)

Derek Robbins, poetry
Sam Simas, prose

spring 2019 (issue 28)

Catherine Pierce, poetry
Sarah Anne Strickley, prose

fall 2018 (issue 27)

Jenny Boychuk, poetry
Farah Ali, prose

spring 2018 (issue 26)

Cindy Tran, poetry
Gianni Skaragas, prose

fall 2017 (issue 25)

Sarah Carson, poetry
Meagan Ciesla, prose

spring 2017 (issue 24)

Ashley Keyser, poetry
Robert Long Foreman, prose

fall 2016 (issue 23)

Tim Carter, poetry
Evelyn Somers, prose

spring 2016 (issue 22)

Bernard Farai Matambo, poetry
Sequoia Nagamatsu, prose

fall 2015 (issue 21)

Jonathan Weinert, poetry
Tyler Mills, prose

spring 2015 (issue 20)

Michelle Oakes, poetry
Donovan Ortega, prose

FORTHCOMING IN AUTUMN 2020

the *Southern* *Review*

POETRY

Paula Abramo *translated by* Dick Cluster, Bonnie Jo Campbell,
John Casteen, Rebecca Morgan Frank, Stephen Gibson, Paul Guest,
David Kirby, Julia B. Levine, Nancy Chen Long, Owen McLeod, Ange Mlinko,
Joel Peckham, Gretchen Steele Pratt, Charles Rafferty, Austen Leah Rosenfeld,
Brandon Rushton, Floyd Skloot, Jane Springer, Joe Wilkins

FICTION

Samar Farah Fitzgerald, Ananda Naima González, John Gu, Steve Trumpeter,
Eva Warrick

NONFICTION

Anna Journey

VISUAL ART

artworks by Leslie Elliottsmith

Subscribe

INDIVIDUALS	INSTITUTIONS
☐ 1 YEAR > $40	☐ 1 YEAR > $90
☐ 2 YEAR > $70	☐ 2 YEAR > $120
☐ 3 YEAR > $90	☐ 3 YEAR > $150
☐ SAMPLE COPY > $12	☐ SAMPLE COPY > $24

For orders outside the U.S. add $18/year for postage and remit in U.S. dollars drawn upon a U.S. bank.
338 Johnston Hall, Louisiana State University, Baton Rouge, LA 70803, USA

New from the UNSUNG MASTERS SERIES

WENDY BATTIN

ON THE LIFE & WORK OF AN AMERICAN MASTER
EDITED BY CHARLES HARTMAN, MARTHA COLLINS,
PAMELA ALEXANDER, & MATTHEW KRAJNIAK

THE UNSUNG MASTERS SERIES

"One of the things I admire most about the poems of Wendy Battin is the strong sense of community, community with the natural world, with geology and geography, with animals and flowers, with the mythic past and women of mythology, with language and fellow poets, with the signs of the stars, with oxygen and alchemy, with many inspired voices, and the wounded among us. Her poems are acts of discovery, often self-discovery, unsparing in both candor and affection."

—ROBERT MORGAN

unsungmasters.org

DEADLINE EXTENDED

the *Missouri Review's*

Jeffrey E. Smith

EDITORS' PRIZE

$5000

per genre

fiction | poetry | nonfiction

OCT 15
deadline

www.missourireview.com

WINNER OF THE **JAKE ADAM YORK PRIZE**

selected by Mark Doty

"Inclusive, generous, both carefully observed and daringly philosophical, these poems reconfigure the elegy for this moment . . ."

—MARK DOTY

"These are poems of the beloved, poems of loss, poems of the body in its many reds . . . I gladly let *In Accelerated Silence* split me open, and a strange thing happened——it stitched me up at the same time."

—MAGGIE SMITH

"Devastating and luminous . . . this book centers on a particular, personal tragedy but resonates beyond into the mysterious galaxy of mourning where were are left unmoored, like planets still orbiting the cold cavities of space where our suns used to burn."

—MATT RASMUSSEN

"For anyone who has ever mourned deeply and loved fiercely, this is your book."

—NICKY BEER

ORDER AT **MILKWEED.ORG**

PRIZE SUBMISSIONS: **COPPER-NICKEL.ORG/BOOKPRIZE**

COPPERNICKEL

subscription rates

For regular folks:

one year (two issues)—$20
two years (four issues)—$35
five years (ten issues)—$60

For student folks:

one year (two issues)—$15
two years (four issues)—$25
five years (ten issues)—$50

For more information, visit: www.copper-nickel.org

To go directly to subscriptions
visit: coppernickel.submittable.com

To order back issues, email wayne.miller@ucdenver.edu